Lost the Plot

Lost the Plot

Finding Our Story in a Confusing World

DAVID S. WISENER

foreword by Amanda Martinez Beck

RESOURCE *Publications* · Eugene, Oregon

LOST THE PLOT
Finding Our Story in a Confusing World

Resource Publications
An Imprint of Wipf and Stock Publishers
199 W. 8th Ave., Suite 3
Eugene, OR 97401

www.wipfandstock.com

PAPERBACK ISBN: 978-1-6667-8323-0
HARDCOVER ISBN: 978-1-6667-8324-7
EBOOK ISBN: 978-1-6667-8325-4

VERSION NUMBER 09/26/23

For my family—past, present, and future—
of which my story is a small part.

CONTENTS

FOREWORD

Stories make us who we are. They help us find meaning in our lives. They highlight our strengths and weaknesses and press on our scars to see how much we have healed. Some have even said that we are human because we seek out meaning through stories. We as humans weave the plot points of our lives together into a tapestry of meaning. And if life can be represented by a tapestry, *Lost the Plot* can be considered the back of a tapestry, full of knots, and full of beauty in its own right. David Wisener turns the tapestry of life and meaning over and begins a dissection—how did I get here and where am I going and how did I get knotted up along the way? *Lost the Plot* holds together these experiences, these stories, and tries to make sense of them while also asking God what the heck God is doing.

As I read *Lost the Plot*, the song "Love Power" from Disney's *Disenchanted* echoed in my mind. It is sung by Idina Menzel, best known as the voice of Elsa. My six-year-old daughter sings it at the top of her lungs whenever it's played on the radio, even though she only knows bits and pieces of the lyrics. She has gotten her bits and pieces lodged into my brain—in fact, the only words from the song that I know are a repetition of "love power" in varying musical arrangements. It occurs to me that there's something powerful here—a theology lesson in snippets from a beloved song: love is the truest form of power to overcome heartache and loss in the world, in my life.

The book you now hold in your hands is a lot like the song "Love Power" to me: in the swelling tide of pain and suffering, David echoes the refrain that love is the ultimate power. But to stop there would discount the breadth of this book. It's not a trite reflection on how God's love overcomes; David struggles with Truth itself to come to his conclusions, much like Jacob wrestling God and walking away with a new name and a limp.

"The world turned upside down" is a lyric from the musical *Hamilton*, describing the victory of American forces over British might. It alludes to the book of Acts, chapter 17, where the disciples of Jesus were accused of turning the world upside down, preaching King Jesus instead of obeying the emperor's decrees. These disciples weren't planning to overthrow the world's military superpower—they were loving the people in front of them and sharing the truth. That's the power of this book—the story of a life turned toward God and toward people. *Lost the Plot* will encourage you to ask questions and wrestle through the answers even as the world is turned upside down around you.

AMANDA MARTINEZ BECK

ACKNOWLEDGMENTS

I thank my immediate family first and foremost for their love, patience, and grace: my dad and mom, Ron and Virginia; brother and sister-in-law, Ronnie and Laura; nieces, Madison and Meagan; and my daughter, Naomi. Likewise my extended family, notably my cousins Brook and Dane, who, despite being separated by several states, were important to me in my teens and early twenties before full adulthood divided our attention. My life wouldn't be right without each of you as part of it.

I'm blessed with several good friends who have helped me in so many ways through the years, even though I'm terrible about staying consistently in touch. You have loved and supported me through highs and lows, and our conversations have molded much of what follows in the pages of this book. At the risk of leaving someone out, in no particular order, I'm mindful of Zachary and Amanda, Jarrod and Rachel, David and Kathleen, David and Lilly, Carter and Karen, Travis and Kelly, Bob, Kenny, Jean-Jacques, Mike. A special thank you to Amanda for writing the foreword to this book—she is the author of two books to date and has an important ministry promoting size-inclusivity and positive body image that I commend to you.

Thanks to all the pastors and Christian leaders who have crossed my path over the years, but in particular to my childhood pastor and his wife, Alan and Chris Patz, who I was blessed to have directly in my life for almost twenty years. You both modeled the love of Jesus with such grace and consistency. I'm thankful for you and humbled by your years of service, patience, and forgiveness.

All glory to God for life, for love, for all things. Thank you for never giving up on me even when I flirted with walking away from you. Help me to finish this race for you, and may my story point others toward you.

EXPOSITION

We were ready to give up when my dad found it. Broken in two, buried upside down in the red Midwestern soil at the back of a small cemetery was my great-great-great grandfather's tombstone. The aged sandstone was caked in layers of dirt and black mold, and his last name was spelled "Wisner."

Dead of unknown causes before his thirtieth birthday, the stone and a few estate papers were the only testaments to his existence. His mother had also died around age thirty, and his older brother passed away four years before him in his early thirties. A genetic disorder? A run of unfortunate family luck? The answer is lost to time.

"Jacob Wisner. Died February 27, 1860. Aged 29 years, 5 months, 18 days."

Nothing more.

As I paused to wipe sweat from my eyes while gazing at the destroyed marker covered by earth in backcountry Ohio, I wondered who will remember me to seek out my resting place 160 years from now.

I'VE BEEN IN LOVE with stories for as long as I can remember. My earliest memories of joy from childhood are connected with my imagination. I loved to play games of make believe, often trying to save the world by fighting titanic battles with a toy sword while running around my house.

When I was four-years-old, I'd ask my mom to write down stories I'd make up on the spot, typically about Transformers (when they were still cool, before Hollywood ruined them). When I learned to write, I'd create characters and jot down my own adventures, invent worlds, and draw comic books.

In third grade, I made my first super hero and showed an early proclivity for alliteration: Drung the Dynamic Defender, a muscled, cape-wearing savior who wore a knight's helmet. In fourth grade, I drew a series of comics featuring my new hero, Water Master, without realizing I'd plagiarized Aquaman.

My other early love was history, maybe because it's the stories we tell of people who came before. I was mesmerized by the ancient civilizations I'd hear about in passing at church, like the Assyrians and Babylonians, so I'd ask my mom to help me read about them in the encyclopedia to learn more about these people and what they did, what they were like.

It turns out stories are important to all of us because they provide our lives with meaning. Whether you realize it or not, you live your life according to several kinds of internalized stories. The tales we believe about ourselves and the world define who we are as people.

When someone asks you to talk about yourself, odds are pretty good you'll talk about your life as a story: where you were born, what your family was like, what you decided to do for a career, your religious beliefs, where you see yourself in the future.

We also don't learn facts about life in a vacuum. We understand them within the framework of a narrative, more readily accepting facts we think support our beliefs and either ignoring, explaining away, or rejecting those that make us call our views into question.

It's in this way that nearly all our lives are controlled by the kinds of stories we believe. We start out life accepting the tales told to us by other people—those in our families, nations, and religions—but as we mature, we begin to choose which stories we accept as reality.

RECENTLY, I'VE FELT LIKE my own story was unravelling. I'm not the man I'd wanted to be when I was young. As a Christian, I'd always thought I'd be doing important things for God and that I'd be successful like I was while growing up.

Instead, I saw my life as littered with failures. I've so far been unsuccessful sustaining any kind of ministry, have largely wandered aimlessly when it comes to a professional career, and haven't been able to maintain a romantic relationship.

I was disillusioned with the American church and its understanding of Christianity, by the people within it who've lost sight of the fact Christ taught us to be humble servants who love others selflessly. We instead too often behave like overlords who seek to force others into living according to our morals in ways that resemble the political methods used by the empires Scripture rebukes.

Like my great-grandfather's headstone, I felt lost, buried, and broken.

But in the death knells of the idea I had of who I am, I've been slowly starting to rewrite my definitions of success, self-understanding, and acceptance.

I've spent a lot of time trying to unravel the stories of God, other people, and myself, and I think it's a journey worth sharing, because the tales we choose to cling to—like the early versions I had of my own story—may be poor reflections of reality and doing us more harm than good.

That applies to almost all of us. I think the broader stories we believe within Western cultures (the cultures of European descent) have been fraying at the edges for hundreds of years, slowly falling apart and starting to collapse.

As a result, our lives are losing their bearings as we drift within different versions of subtly nihilistic narratives. We would all do well to examine the stories we buy into and to peer more closely at and ask ourselves probing questions about them.

That's the adventure I'd like to take with you in the pages that follow, as I share my life, the stories I've believed, and the thoughts I've had throughout different parts of it.

We'll look at my experiences with Christianity and the church; explore why we think in the ways we do and see reality differently; examine our shared heritage as both children of the West and, for many of us, of America; look more deeply into what love is and what the hardships of life mean; and follow between chapters the progression of my personal story as a metaphor, a microcosm of the larger tales we hold to.

I've been wrong a lot, and I bet you probably have been, too. The fact is, a lot of the stories we've believed aren't actually true, and not in some malicious way, but because in our innocence we can be gullible.

I assumed the seemingly-idyllic, rural northern Florida I grew up in had always been peaceful and relatively prosperous. The friendly small towns and tranquil land today give no indication that 120 years ago they were the center of a large network of prison work camps that abused and killed convicts in the rape of the land for phosphate.

It's a story that's glossed over by local historians for obvious reasons. The thickly-wooded gorges and ravines I ran through as a child were once mining pits where men, women, and children were forced labor in an industry that was responsible for the establishment of several of the communities I know so well.

An exposé by a Brooklyn newspaper in 1900; the death of a boy that made national news in 1903; and the memoirs of a former prison guard likening the camps to an "American Siberia" eventually contributed to the demise of the work-lease programs used as convict slave labor, but the memories and the spiritual heritage that hang over the land remain in need of healing.

Just as we all do. We all need healing from the trauma that's been inflicted on us and from the damage we've dealt, whether we think we do or not. It sits with us and festers like a wound unless it's dealt with, corrupting our personal stories and our souls.

Healing. Redemption. Central aspects to the Christian story of existence, the story I've imperfectly understood but clung to since childhood, and the story whose reformation in my heart and mind has been setting me free.

It was in that spirit that, a couple years after unearthing my great-grandfather's tombstone, I returned to Ohio to see what I could do about restoring it.

1

FOUNDATIONS AND MEANING

amily has played an important role in my journey to understand how we become the kinds of people we are. How does your family affect who you are? Can events from the past still impact the present?

Each of us is a unique mix of countless ancestors in our mother's and father's families, our DNA forming our human "hardware," so to speak. That's the "nature" part of us, and the "nurture" part—how we're raised by our families during our formative years—is usually held responsible for what makes up our human "software": our opinions, beliefs, and personalities.

But it turns out genetics also affects us in ways that had been attributed to nurture. Epigenetics is a young science, but it's produced evidence that our experiences in life change the expression of our genes in ways that are passed on to our children. In other words, when we go through a trauma, there are observable changes to our cells as a result.

That suggests that the converse may also be true, that actions you and I take today can slowly help to heal the hurts and genetic alterations our ancestors experienced so that we and our children can begin to recover from traumas we inherited from the past.

In my curiosity to learn more about my family, I began to make deeper connections within myself. I've been able to recognize themes in my life that are echoes from the past. My hope is that I can bring some bit of redemption to the hurts in the multigenerational tale of which I'm a part.

As I've learned of the humble origins of my paternal family, stories have emerged that call for healing. I'm told my grandfather, who passed away before I was born, could be a stern man, which is not surprising for a farmer who lived during the Great Depression in rural Indiana. As one of eleven siblings, I have a massive extended family.

Yet I only know people from a few of those siblings, in large part due to a grievance among several which resulted in them no longer associating with each other. It's tragic and troubling that brothers and sisters could choose to cut each other out of their lives, and I sense a lingering predisposition within myself that could be an echo of those inclinations.

Tracing back further, it becomes clear that the succeeding generations from my great-grandfather to my grandfather and then my father mellowed in several ways. Only vague, negative overtones are recalled of my great-great grandfather, and his father, of course, is the mysterious owner of the prodigal tombstone I seek to restore.

My fourth and fifth great-grandfathers were Quakers, and my fifth brought his family from South Carolina to Western Ohio as part of a Quaker settlement. My sixth great-grandfather was one of five brothers, sons of my seventh great-grandfather, Jacob, who came to America in 1749 from the small village of Bubendorf, Switzerland.

Settling in northern South Carolina in the 1750s, he and his family became victims of the Revolutionary War. At least one of his sons was an active Tory in local militias. There was a lot of fighting in the area where his family lived, likened by historians to the equivalent of a civil war between neighbors.

It's been difficult to learn much about Jacob and his sons outside of South Carolina land records, and his sons eventually went separate ways and lost touch with one another, quite possibly to escape infamy amongst their neighbors for having supported the English Crown during the War. No related Wiseners seem to have remained in South Carolina following the early 1800s.

Even before setting foot in America, Jacob was banished upon leaving his native village, a place where the Wiseners had lived for hundreds of years. People were so heavily discouraged from emigrating at the time that, once they made the decision to leave, they were banned from ever returning.

Many of the issues the generations of my paternal family wrestled with seem to be variations on similar themes: struggle, a feeling of disconnection, a sense of not belonging, and sensitivity to grievances and perceived injustices.

By learning my family's story, I can try to heal the broken places. I can pass on the tales and the tragedies of members choosing to disassociate, and I can refuse to do so myself. I can choose to remain connected, and I can encourage my family members to do the same. I can do my best to ensure the feelings of abandonment and not being able to return home that reverberate in my bones are redeemed.

Ultimately, healing is about being healthy human beings. It's about wrestling with weaknesses, whether those are personal or inherited, and refusing to be victimized by them. It's about seeking wholeness, seeking peace, and spreading that shalom wherever we are.

LET'S LOOK CLOSER AT how we understand facts and develop meaning.

A plant I've had since I was three-years-old is suddenly blooming for the first time in my life. That is a fact. But my brain keeps working, because I'll probably think about what that fact means: this plant has never produced a flower; now it has; perhaps this is a sign of something good. Or, alternatively, I could think:

this plant has never produced a flower; now it has; it's just a coincidence with no deeper meaning.

Those two options broadly represent the two prominent choices we in Western societies choose between when giving meaning to events. Notice that both views don't deny the facts: a plant has never flowered; now it has. But the facts by themselves don't lead to meaning. Facts don't answer, "Why now?" Why did events only now produce this result?

This is a silly example, but it illustrates the point fairly well: our choice to explain events within specific meaning-stories—metanarratives, to use the philosophical term—comes mainly from our backgrounds and our demeanor.

Across the many kinds of metanarratives (and there are several, such as atheist, Buddhist, Muslim, pantheist, agnostic, Jewish, Christian, humanist, and so on) there seems to be a common theme that resonates: love.

Even if we think love is just a side effect of evolution, we still shape a lot of our lives around it. Even if we think love is only an illusion, it's still a large part of life for people who otherwise seek to rid themselves of all desire. There is no escaping love.

That said, it makes sense if there is some sort of personality behind the existence of the universe that love would likewise be important to it.

I think it's fair to say, of the major metanarratives, love is most central in the Christian story. That doesn't mean love isn't important in other metanarratives, but only that it isn't as vital to the essence of the story as it is within Christianity.

Christianity is incomprehensible without love. It is centered on the person of Jesus of Nazareth, a Jewish religious teacher from early first-century Palestine who taught an upside-down version of who God is and what God is concerned about compared to what was taught by the religious establishment at the time. Jesus claimed to be the long-prophesied Jewish messiah, the savior of Israel, and also God incarnate in human form.

The emphasis of Jesus' teaching focused on God's reckless love for humanity. The Christian understanding of Jesus' death at the hands of Roman imperial and Jewish religious powers is as an act of God taking upon himself the darkness of existence—injustice, oppression, pride, greed—in order to redeem creation because of love. The resurrection is the evidence that this redemption is in motion.

Love is God's motivation, love is God's purpose, and love is Jesus' primary command to those who would follow him (see John 13:34–35).

The Christian story resonates with me. In my experience, love is the best thing about life, and the love expressed within Christianity (self-sacrificial; committed; persevering; humble) is the purest love I know. That's why I find Christianity compelling philosophically.

Of course, that doesn't address its factual claims. But if I were to believe in a god not of my own making, that God is one that I would follow. That is a God who speaks to life as I actually experience it, whether I can fully understand him or not.

BUT WHAT DOES IT mean to be a Christian? What is it that makes a person one?

No surprise, the answer depends on what kind of Christian you ask. I'm going to try to provide the answer I think Jesus and his apostles would have given, though to be fair, if asked, every kind of Christian would probably think he or she is doing the same thing.

Very broadly, the term "Christian" translates in Greek to "little Christ," which suggests those who identified as Christians were attempting to model themselves after Jesus Christ. A Christian, then, is one who tries to be like, or follow, Jesus.

But lots of people claim to follow Jesus and go in a million different directions. Is there a right way to follow Jesus, and what does it mean to follow him in the first place?

A basic way to follow someone is to do what he or she says. Jesus himself says in John 14:15, "If you love me, you will keep my commands." The only records of what Christ said are the written New Testament Gospels of Matthew, Mark, Luke, and John, and those, it is widely agreed, were written decades after Jesus' crucifixion.

So we depend on tradition to determine what Jesus said and what he meant. Oral tradition carried the gospel stories for many years, after which the Christian church has passed down the written stories for 1,900 years. Most of the other books of the New Testament expand on the Gospel accounts to explain what the apostles understood about Christ, the human condition, and the church.

Yet not everyone agrees on how to understand and interpret the New Testament. It was written thousands of years ago in a vastly different culture by several authors. So we rely on orthodox traditions of the church, our scholarly methods of analysis, and God's guidance to explain the meaning of the texts.

What, then, is the bottom line? What is salvation for a Christian, and what does it take? Christians believe all of humanity struggles with sin, which is best understood as a tendency to rebel against God. Humanity's original decision to rebel in ages past tainted all of creation—sin is corrupting by nature, so it altered the state of all life, introducing disease, decay, and death. Because sin is rebellion against God, it also damaged the relationship between God and people. So to restore that relationship and reverse the destructive effects of sin, humanity needed a cure, something to save us.

Christians believe Jesus provides that salvation, but how precisely he does so has, unfortunately, been described as nothing more than a legal transaction in many Christian circles: I intellectually believe Jesus lived a sinless life and died as a kind of sacrifice for my sins, then God the Father counts Christ's sinlessness as my own, and then I go to heaven when I die.

That is, to put it kindly, incomplete. And generally misleading. The New Testament epistles are filled with examples of the apostle Paul telling Christians to live life in a holy way, to run the race of life in a way that ensures we will finish what we started. In other words, there's a much larger dimension at play in the Christian life than merely accepting an intellectual belief.

Take it from a favorite contemporary Christian author, Dallas Willard, from his book *The Divine Conspiracy*:

> If you ask any . . . American who says they have made a commitment to Jesus Christ what the Christian gospel is, you will probably be told that Jesus died to pay for our sins, and that if we will only believe he did this, we will go to heaven when we die…What must be emphasized in all of this is the difference between trusting Christ, the real person Jesus, with all that that naturally involves, versus trusting some arrangement for sin-remission set up through him—trusting only his role as guilt remover. To trust the real person Jesus is to have confidence in him in every dimension of our real life, to believe that he is right about and adequate to everything.

A Christian is a follower of Christ by following Jesus the person and trusting him. By following his commands. By trusting those he left in control of his church.

That is what it means to be saved—to begin living the new life God has made available through following his incarnate son right now. Salvation begins right now, not later in heaven. It's a life transformed by and submitted to Christ until we breathe our last breath.

The transformation is never complete in this life, but we move closer through the power of God himself, through his Holy Spirit. And there is grace and mercy when we fall short.

But it is the intent of the heart in submission to Christ, demonstrated by our life that is lived in response, which marks those who are truly "little Christs."

A FAULTY VIEW OF Jesus, though, will derail a true understanding of the story told by Christianity. It has, in the past, threatened damage to my trust in God.

I risk getting ahead of myself, but I remember a crisis of faith I had in my mid-twenties that will be described in more detail a bit later on. My trouble centered on whether there was any point to me continuing with the faith. I wanted a deeper connection to God than what's on offer in most American churches.

It seems to me Jesus is often portrayed by Christians as a superhero, which creates an aura around him like a Greek god. That defeats part of the purpose Christians believe God became a human, though, which was to make himself more tangible and knowable.

The orthodox Christian teaching is Jesus of Nazareth is both fully God and fully man. Superhero Jesus seemed in tune with the God part but not the man. I felt if I was to worship him and model my life after his, then I best well figure out the depths of who he was and is.

It's important to embrace Jesus as completely human. He laughed. He cried. He smiled. He became angry. He had a sense of humor. He stubbed his toes. He was precocious as a child. He was a carpenter until he began his ministry at around age thirty.

He must have been passionate about his beliefs and a charismatic speaker to attract the following he did. One can believe he was sinless while still leaving room for him to have had doubts, concerns, and an awareness of his sexuality.

Paul was emphatic in his letter to the Philippian church that Jesus, though the Son of God, did not take advantage of the benefits of God, but rather lived just like any one of us (Phil 2:5–8). He wasn't equivalent to a superhero (though there are moments in Scripture that do testify to his unique glory, such as the Holy Spirit descending on him at his baptism [Luke 3:22] and his transfiguration [Matt 17:1–8]). Jesus even said that everything he did, we can do, too (John 14:12).

He lived in constant communication with God the Father, and the insights he had into his life and the lives of others were whatever the Father revealed to him. He didn't know the future, and he couldn't read peoples' minds beyond what the Father showed him. The miracles he performed were done by relying on the indwelling of the Holy Spirit, the same indwelling that the disciples received at Pentecost after Jesus' resurrection and ascension.

He had some level of self-awareness regarding his identity and destiny on the cross. Yet, while he trusted the Father, he had to have had some doubt. His panic in the garden of Gethsemane prior to his arrest becomes more tragically beautiful when I see I can relate—in some small way—with his stress, begging the Father that he wouldn't have to do what he thought he must, which would result in his death.

When I realize Jesus experienced life like I do and sacrificed his own wants and desires in order to do what the Father wanted, I am drawn to him. When I understand that God as Trinity (three distinct persons yet one being united in essence: the Father, the Son, and the Holy Spirit) chose to tie himself willingly to his creation by living life as a creature and pulling humanity into his own essence, I see beauty.

A God who chooses solidarity with his creation and chooses to experience existence on its terms is a God who intimately and deeply cares and loves. I look at Jesus, and I see not only the second person of the Trinity in human form, but I also see a man who understands the same temptations, trials, and struggles I know so well.

And the more intimately I know him, the more I want to be like him.

2

WRESTLING WITH CHRISTIANITY

We've all been hurt in life. We all have a hole in our heart that's aching to be filled. Christian theology traces the emptiness inside us back to the Fall—the shattering of humanity's relationship with God through our decision to sin as told in Genesis—made worse by the scars we collect as life goes on.

How to allow God to heal our wounds is hard to describe. It's more a process of developing an intimate relationship with him than it is a step-by-step check list, and it sure seems to me like most American Christians have lost touch with this intimacy. We're more interested in using God's name to champion our political causes and justify our opinions and actions.

My experience with trying to heal my wounded heart with whatever quick-fix bandage I could find goes back to early childhood. Affirmation and achievement have long acted like drugs that make me feel better about myself. From always being seen as a good kid by adults to finding a niche in school as an accomplished nerd, I thrived on receiving the approval of others, winning, and coming out on top.

As I grew into a teenager, I began to try to find a girl who could be my soul mate. I was obsessed with getting married. It seemed a romantic relationship was a natural place to look for fulfillment since they're the main focus of our pop culture.

This particular idol has faded in luster over the years, though, as I've managed to make a pretty fine mess out of the handful of close romantic relationships I've had, which has served as a wake-up call to what my deeper motivations likely were.

But winning—I like to win. Not just at games, but also at life: having the best ideas, being the most-thorough thinker, making an actual difference in the world. I ate up the possibilities in my late teens when I finished at the top of my high school class, won academic awards, and enjoyed the general approval of family, friends, and local community. As they say, the world was my oyster—minus athletic skills, I was an All-American kid.

Ah, but life. My demons—of which more will be said—were always there, hiding in the background. But as long as I kept winning, they stayed in the dark. And I was determined to win. I *would* change the world, I *would* make a difference, I *would* be acknowledged as someone people needed.

The only trouble with all that is, well, eventually, we all lose. And the thing is, when I finally lost, I understood I was to blame, because of who I was as a person and the choices I'd made. I struggled to reconcile that reality with the self-image I'd crafted.

Emotionally, my heart was hurt by the loss of love the summer after high school, when my first romantic relationship fell apart and left me gutted. Intellectually, I left the pond of my small-town community and met many people who were much more intelligent and talented than I was.

It's also unfortunate to be in college and have no idea what you want to do with yourself. Since the carpentry thing wasn't for me, what's the major one should choose to be Savior of the World?

Suddenly my ideals at the end of high school came crashing into the malaise of a life with few certainties. I'd discarded my love of history in middle school since I decided the Path to Importance didn't go that way. So, I coasted by in life.

Then, while trudging through an undergraduate degree, God seemingly stepped in and gave me a calling. Through several random events, I found myself helping lead worship in my church while also serving as the director of youth ministries—at the age of twenty-one. Surely this would be how I began to leave Billy Graham in the dust.

It went well for a couple years, but, goodness, it was hard on my emotions and spirituality. I had no idea how to rely on the Holy Spirit to sustain me. Trying to finish my degree, leading several classes and ministries, and still trying to have some sort of social life took its toll.

I poured myself out in service and in pursuit of accomplishments but didn't have a clue how to refill what I gave away. I begged God for help, but he didn't seem to answer. I prayed for strength, for clarity, for determination, for increased holiness, for more motivation, and all I received was—I thought—silence. I imploded.

What followed was a period of life I've been ashamed of. I resigned from my ministry positions abruptly, and I started a romantic relationship I never should have. Self-forgiveness has been difficult because of how I hurt and disappointed several people.

Church was dead to me. God seemed silent, and I was growing frustrated with worship that was trying too hard to look like a rock concert. I graduated college with what seemed like a useless degree and no clue what I was going to do next.

Through fits and starts my life since has been about trying to find out who I actually am in God. About repairing as best I can the damage done in my early-twenties. About finding out whether there is any meat to this Christianity thing or if it's just a giant social club. About finding God as a person and not just an idea, and finally about giving him my life to do with what he wants—for his sake and not my own.

It's that last sentence that's really frustrating, because I'd believed that's what my life had been devoted to for a long time. But it wasn't. Much like my critique of the American church, it was about what I wanted in God's name. The franchises I wanted to start and have God bless.

And therein lies the irony of Christian humility for me. I'd wanted to be someone important for the Kingdom of God, but if God was ever going to use me effectively, it meant I actually did have to go through that whole dying to self thing Jesus talks a lot about. The reality of a faith whose champions are the persecuted and marginalized was nonetheless still a shock to me, someone who desperately wanted to think highly of himself in certain ways.

The depths of the death to self shocked me. I mean, this isn't just a word we toss around here, "death." It meant the old standards, the old ways of doing life (yes, even many of the ways I'd picked up from other Christians) had to go.

All those words I'd heard for so many years actually had bite to them for the first time. We have to be humbled, to be brought low and to realize that, goodness, none of this life really has to do with anything intrinsic in you or me, other than the fact God loves us just as we are.

And humbling hurts. Being emptied of all the pretenses, ambitions, and dreams that we're raised from birth in this culture to follow as if they're some Manifest Destiny to the Glory of the Self hurts.

As we begin to allow ourselves to be emptied and discipled into ways of developing a corporate and individual relationship with the person of God, this is when we begin to see where those Christians in the New Testament were coming from.

Scripture as the collective memory of God's people does actually prove to be useful in helping us remember who God is and how he meets us. And that's just the thing—the power of Christianity in its beginnings was the power of its experience: this stuff really did work for people. If it didn't, there's no way the religion would have survived.

Paul told folks to witness for themselves: "We saw Jesus raised from the dead. But it wasn't just me—there were about 500 of us he appeared to, and they're still around, go ask them" (1 Cor 15:3–8, my paraphrase).

Christianity at its best is still the same—God shows up, come and see. No, really. But to grow as a Christian means that one must be brought low, emptied of self, and filled with the Holy Spirit.

It isn't an easy decision to make. God is still dragging me a good bit of the way. But ultimately, it's about taking his hand and walking with him wherever he goes, filled with his peace and love in ways more real than that trite saying can express.

I choose to trust as best I can and carry on.

I THINK MY DISILLUSIONMENT with the church centers on how it frames what Christianity is and what it means to be a Christian.

I'm a theology nerd, so I love discussions and debates about the nature of God and the church, but I think we've valued having head knowledge about God over heart knowledge to the point that a large number of us, maybe even most of us, don't realize there is more to being a Christian than believing the right ideas about God.

We've neutered Christianity to the point that it's become about believing certain ideas, and that's it.

That's never been what Christianity is. The heart of Christianity is a radical transformation of an entire person through his or her encounters with God and intentional training in a new way of being human molded on the pattern of Jesus of Nazareth.

It's about the experience of knowing God, of knowing Christ, bowing our knee, and allowing God to rewrite everything we thought we knew and everything we thought we were as humans. Right belief is important, but it is far, far from being everything.

We have to experience God, to rest in the presence of God, to be saturated by God—we have to feel God in our bones, not only believe ideas in our heads. And we have to allow God the room to correct us, to help us realize we were wrong about how to understand Jesus, how to understand humanity, how to understand many aspects of life.

If we aren't radically challenged by engaging the teachings of Christ and engaging God directly, then we aren't doing it right.

We've abandoned discipleship and sanctification, abandoned the possibility of experiencing the divine.

If I hadn't had my own experiences of God's presence to rely on, I might have left Christianity a long time ago, but much of the church acts as if those experiences either aren't possible or aren't important. Even the best of our churches, the ones who encourage encountering God, often leave us at that point, leaving it up to us to figure it out from there, as if Jesus and the church didn't leave pretty detailed accounts of the church's responsibility and role in actively discipling us.

Instead, we've limited the church to just being a place in which we show up once a week to be lectured and maybe take communion before going about life as usual.

It's supposed to be a group of people that we regularly share life with and are intentionally shaping us into looking more like Jesus through our thoughts, our actions, and the way we engage the world. It's supposed to be challenging, to require effort.

In our laziness or in our fear of offending, we've abdicated these responsibilities. We've become echo chambers for repeating our versions of who Jesus and God are—either hucksters of a distorted idea of freedom and America on one extreme or enablers and hyper-relativists on the other—and not allowed our God and our traditions to challenge everything we think we know.

Because we've largely become social clubs instead of places of divine encounter through rituals that guide radical self-transformation, people are understandably leaving. They see our hypocrisy and our unwillingness to challenge ourselves and take ownership and accountability and, most damningly, try to continually become better human beings.

I can't blame them for wanting nothing to do with that: neither do I.

And look, I'm no model of an ideal Christian—while I ache for authentic discipleship, I likewise am scared to death of it because I know just how hard it is. I've too often distanced myself from the church instead of more actively trying to be an agent of change within it. None of us are free from hypocrisy, but that doesn't make any of this less true.

The church needs to repent and, well, come to Jesus. We need to strive to know him for who he truly is and not the Idol in Jesus-clothing we've likely thought him to be, the Jesus who acts as a god for our personal desires and agendas.

We need to tell everyone that the point of Christianity is in entering into and experiencing life with God that includes divine encounters and results in a radical change in what it means to be human. And we need to disciple and lovingly hold people accountable in their journey to becoming more like Christ.

Only this level of authenticity, reclaiming of our original purpose, and reliance on the power of God can save us.

WHEN YOU THINK ABOUT it, though, it's weird that people choose to be Christian, isn't it? To follow the teachings of a guy who lived 2,000 years ago among a minority cultural group on the margins. To associate with a religion that is often synonymous with modern-day American zealotry.

Why would anyone, myself included, drink that Kool Aid? I was born into the church, but I've chosen to continue being Christian as an adult, despite doubts, frustrations, and uncertainty. Why?

For one, I find it to be beautiful. That's no justification in itself, but I have to admit I want Christianity to be true. Where German philosopher Friedrich Nietzsche despised a religion he thought championed weakness and failure, I celebrate one that recognizes love requires sacrifice; that teaches that in serving others and denying selfishness, I surprisingly find life.

But while that may be well and good, you can appreciate those things and still think Christianity isn't true. There are plenty of beautiful religions and philosophies—I find aspects of Hinduism moving and poetic, but I'm not a Hindu. Likewise, plenty of people admire Jesus but think it's ridiculous any human could be God.

So, again, why? Why believe a would-be Jewish messiah is God in human form? In part, because of the way I understand history and how that helps me make sense of my life experiences.

Christianity is unique from a lot of religions and philosophies because it depends on history. If a single historical event—the resurrection—didn't happen, Christian theology would collapse. If Jesus didn't rise from the dead, he remains a fascinating teacher, but the belief he is divine is a great hoax. If he died and stayed dead like, well, people do, then it's a pretty safe bet he was just another dude.

And it's an outrageous claim—a man died, was dead for three days, then, poof: not dead. So why believe a dead man came to life?

As N.T. Wright explains in his book *The Resurrection of the Son of God*, the undeniable historical event that has to be explained is how in the heck Christianity even exists. We don't have an answer for how it gained traction and took over much of the religious world unless the resurrection actually happened.

There were a whole lot of guys who claimed to be the Jewish messiah back in the day. Without exception, all of them failed— the Romans killed them one way or another, usually at the end of a failed rebellion.

If you were Jewish and had followed a failed messiah, you would look for another one to throw off the Roman yoke. It happened quite a few times until Rome had enough and raised Jerusalem to the ground in 70 CE.

Jesus was an outlier to other would-be messiahs. First, he didn't talk about the Roman occupation. Second, he didn't want to start a military revolution against Rome. Third, it seems he claimed to be divine, which is definitely not compatible with Judaism. Fourth, he died in disgrace, arrested without a fuss and executed by the state in a manner offensive to Jewish custom.

Then, unlike the followers of other supposed messiahs, his disciples didn't go searching for a new one—they claimed he came back to life. They talked to him, saw him, touched him, ate with him, and said he told them to institute the Kingdom of God on earth through peaceful means.

If you were someone witnessing these first Christians, you probably thought they're nuts.

So, prove them wrong. Produce Jesus' dead body.

But it's gone. Can't find it.

OK, so his followers must have stolen it as a hoax.

But they're being persecuted. They have no respect, they have no power, they have no money. They end up being tortured and killed. People die for something they believe is true, but who would do that to themselves and their families over something they knew was a lie?

OK, so the disciples honestly believe he is alive again, but it's only a few who actually claim to have seen him alive, and maybe they're hallucinating, and everyone else is just going along.

But it's more than a few. They claim Jesus appeared to over 500 of them at the same time and stayed with them for forty days (Acts 1:3), and they're encouraging everyone to verify it, to talk directly to those who have been with him.

OK, well, maybe he wasn't really killed on the cross. Maybe he just passed out and woke up after three days.

But the Romans are pretty good at this crucifixion deal—they do it a lot. They know how to kill people and make sure they're dead, especially someone they kill on charges of being a political threat. Plus, a not-quite-dead Jesus emerging from a tomb in three days is not going to convince anyone he has defeated death if he looks like death itself, and his disciples say his body was glorified, and only scars remain from the nails.

The historical argument boils down to this: we have to explain how a group of ordinary Jewish men and women became convinced a horribly disgraced, failed messiah was God-made-man and had physically come back from death.

Their enemies—and there were plenty—couldn't prove them wrong because they couldn't produce a body, and more than that, because the disciples swore he was alive and glorified.

On top of that, how did these disciples start what became the world's largest religion? Most weren't educated, and they didn't have motivations like power, prestige, or political control. These were ordinary fishermen and peasants.

But that by itself is still not why I'm a Christian. Because even if I grant that, it has no impact on my life right now. Jesus rose from the dead; so what? The world still stinks, my life is still confusing, and a lot of horrible things still happen. What gives?

I don't have a perfect answer. I still struggle with it and probably always will. But I know if you look at the problem of evil in a different way, it could be posed as the problem of good. Instead of asking "Why does evil exist?" it's an equally fair and confusing question to ask "Why does good exist?" Why do we assume life should be good, and why are there good things in life? If evil is confusing, so is goodness.

But that's just philosophy. What about real, tangible life?

There's an open secret out there we in Western cultures like to sweep under the rug: weird stuff happens. Unexplainable things happen every day. And, sure, we can tell ourselves that what is confusing today is only waiting to be explained by science tomorrow, and there's truth to that.

But theories in quantum physics hold that reality is made up of dimensions beyond the physical in which the laws of science as we know them don't apply—there are different rules at work that are nonetheless present and seemingly unexplainable all around us.

Christianity makes sense to me of the life I've lived and what I've seen.

A bishop I know told the story of a friend who was scheduled to have his arteries cleared of blockage. His friend prayed that God would make his arteries as clear as a baby's, even though every adult has some plaque and blockage. At his next doctor's appointment, the doctor informed him he no longer needed the procedure because he literally had no blockage—his arteries were as clear as a baby's. The bishop called it a miracle. The doctor said it was just an anomaly. He asked the doctor how often he sees anomalies, and the doctor replied, "I see anomalies every day."

And of course, for every testimony of answered prayer, there are a thousand seemingly unanswered—someone asked for God's help, and looks like God didn't show up. I can't explain that any more than I can explain why some miracles do happen.

One strange truth is the human mind is sometimes able to influence healing simply by believing something to be true—the power of our thoughts can and do impact our physical condition.

Not all the stories of miracles I've heard and seen can be attributed to the mind, though. People have been prayed for by others without knowing they were receiving prayer and been healed of cancer and other diseases. This stuff happens. Miracles (anomalies) are real—how do we explain them?

I'm a Christian because my mind and my heart point me to the cross. Because so much of life is upside down and hard to understand that, if God is real, I would expect him to be similar.

My experience and heart affirm that the kind of love demonstrated by Jesus—sacrificial, committed, determined, persevering—*that's* love that makes it in this life. That's how I want to be loved, and that's how I want to love.

That's a vision of life and love worth dying for.

WHEN WORKING ON MY family tree, whenever I discover a new ancestor, I'm reminded that, eventually, no one will remember me. As the years melt by when I'm dead and buried and the generations multiply, someday there won't be a soul around who even remembers I was once real.

It's depressing stuff.

It's another reason I hope in the Christian faith—a hope that rests in everything about us meaning something eternally. The things we do and say while we're alive ripple and echo beyond just ourselves, impacting countless others through butterfly effects so subtle and small yet so potentially profound that we're truly changing the course of humanity every day of our lives.

But there's an even deeper beauty to the Christian hope and what it means to who we are. Our actions are more critical to defining ourselves than many Christians realize.

Because, who are we, really? From a Christian perspective, are we defined by the sum of all our past experiences coming together at any single point in time we choose to call "the present"? If I were to die this instant, would the person I am at the moment of death be who I am in eternity?

I'd argue that isn't so. If that were true, it privileges a single moment of the present at the expense of all the moments from our past, which make up by far the fuller story of who each of us is.

The Christian often belittles the past in the name of moving beyond the mistakes we've made, and, true enough, our growth is important. But ironically, we cheapen forgiveness and grace by downplaying the importance of our past, and we abuse the fact God always offers them to us. That leads to us not living our lives as if our actions in each present moment matter.

On the contrary, who I am *now* . . . and *now* . . . and *now* . . . in every present moment, taken altogether, is the full reality of who I am.

That doesn't mean there is no forgiveness for mistakes, or that people can't change, but that the present should be filled with a greater sense of seriousness than the typical Christian gives it, the Christian who holds back giving full effort in discipleship due to resting in the assurance of future grace and forgiveness.

Because if God is God and this thing of life we're doing means what we think it means, then when I stand before the judgment throne at the end of history, it will be at the end of time as we know it, because time is a creation of God like everything else in our universe. I will stand not as the person I am in that instant, but as every person I've ever been in every moment of my life.

I own my past more than simply baggage to lug around—it's truly me, just as much as the me you know today is, even though that guy is different than he was ten years ago.

That's both comforting and terrifying, but it should lead us to treat our actions as more important than we often do. I've rested on the belief I'm free to mess up because God will forgive me, but—while true—that's immature Christianity and ignorant of what I'm building in my life.

That little boy thirty years ago is still real and part of me, more than in just a figurative sense. That young and immature twenty-something who did more damage than he realized is likewise still real and part of me.

The good news about that is, despite how we mess up, sanctification and redemption work on all of who we are—they work retroactively and free us from the guilt and condemnation of what we've done while at the same time not erasing it.

The true Christian perspective on daily life should therefore be one not scared of making mistakes, but also not one all-too-willing to do so because we know forgiveness is right there whenever we want it.

Every moment we leave behind, every memory, is eternal and not ephemeral. They matter, whether we have pictures to remember them by or whether they fade out of all human memory. Each of them is part of who we eternally are.

RISING ACTION

You might not think a 160-year-old, broken tombstone would be all that heavy, but you'd be wrong. It was a warm summer day when I journeyed back out to the cemetery where my third great-grandfather was buried. The drive is peaceful down old country roads to the resting place of a long-vanished community.

Ghosts echo across the plains of the Midwest in old, rundown buildings and churches dotting the landscape. For those who pay attention, the number of cemeteries whisper the truth: the dead outnumber the living. Farming isn't as common as it once was in America, so those communities are shells of their former selves, many of their sons and daughters having left decades ago.

My great-grandfather's resting place lies across from a salvage yard, backed up to rusted-out cars and trucks. A dog barks at me when I walk up to the old, broken stone, but soon enough leaves me alone with my shovel and my thoughts.

It doesn't take much prying to pull up the two large pieces of the tombstone, but I'm on the lookout for smaller parts that would be important in putting it back together. No such luck. But I do spot, through a random glance, what looks like a slot buried in the earth.

Some light digging uncovers the relic: a footer for the headstone, marking the exact location where my great-grandfather lies. I smile, knowing I won't have to guess where his remains are, and if my restoration is a success, his stone has an official home.

Digging up the footer is another matter entirely, but, after a lot of sweat and over an hour's labor, the remains of the tombstone and the footer are resting on cloth in the back of my rental car.

I'm thankful this is rural America and no one is around to ask me awkward questions about why I'm stealing an old marker.

I WAS BORN AND raised to a middle class, Christian family during the early 1980s in rural north Florida.

My dad is from Indiana, where most of his family remains, but he moved to Florida with his parents in the 1950s. He taught high school science for over thirty years.

My mom was born in Miami and grew up in south Florida, and most of her family has been in the state since the mid-1800s. She always wanted to be a mom, so when she became one, she stayed at home to raise my brother and me.

I was a late surprise addition to my family. My dad was forty-four and my mom a week shy of forty when I was born, and my older brother was thirteen. That's how a Millennial was raised by a dad who grew up during the end of the Depression and a mom who epitomizes the vestige of a southern lady.

My earliest memories of life are of feelings of foreboding, hesitation, and fear, despite being told I was a happy baby and toddler.

I had trouble sleeping and clung to my mother for safety and comfort. The impressions I recall of my early years are of being frightened at night, and of sometimes sensing just a heavy, melancholy weight around me.

But I adored my older brother. I can remember jumping in bed with him in the morning as he pretended to be asleep still while I giggled trying to wake him up. I can still feel the remains of the affection I developed for him from those early years within my heart as he was very much a second father figure for me.

Fear dogged me in different ways from the earliest of ages, as I was scared of anything that made a loud noise. My mom says that late in her pregnancy with me, she was at a train station picking up my grandmother when a whistle screamed loudly, and I flipped in her womb. My parents bought me a tiny electric four-wheel car when I must have been three or four, and it was too loud for me to drive very much.

I recall that was an early disappointment to my brother as he loved cars, motorcycles, and anything that was fast.

My dad has been a rock in his presence, though early on he was busy teaching night classes and running a small construction company with my mom on the side to make extra money, so he was often distracted.

My mom remains my role model in love—since she stayed at home, I spent most of my time with her, and she was emotionally present and engaged with me, always loving and caring with me and everyone she encountered.

Another clear early memory is anger. I had a bad temper, though it wasn't frequently aroused. I can't tell you why, but when something I cared about didn't go my way, I would feel deep resentment—like a feeling of injustice had been committed against the universe—that would just well up inside me with intense emotion.

When I was six, my brother married young to his high school sweetheart, and though they lived nearby, I guess in hindsight it was like I lost a father, since I no longer spent nearly the same amount of time with him as I once did.

I also began to feel more deeply like I was a disappointment to him because he couldn't seem to understand how I wasn't interested in the same sorts of things he was. I'd rather read books and play using my imagination than ride dirt bikes or go-carts.

It was at the age of seven that my world imploded inside my own head. I began having intense panic attacks that would last several hours every night.

I had become very goal-oriented at school, determined to be successful so I could do whatever I wanted to when I was an adult. But I became aware that I could sabotage my own goals—if I wasn't able to get the sleep I needed at night, I wouldn't be able to be successful in school, which would result in becoming what I saw as a failure as an adult.

So I panicked—I *had* to get good sleep. And, of course, that resulted in me not being able to relax to rest.

It's hard to describe the panic cycle to someone who hasn't experienced it. Your own mind really does become your worst enemy. And you fully recognize that, which makes it worse.

You get caught in a series of repeating negative thoughts that you feel powerless to stop. Your fears, in the form of your own thoughts, become very real things, almost tangible. A fear manifests itself (I can't sleep), which causes a physical response (nausea) that you're likewise afraid of and don't want to experience, which reinforces the original fear, which reinforces the physical response. Repeat.

My breath would get short as I lay in bed. I would become incredibly nauseated, my body's natural stress response.

As these episodes kept happening night after night, I became super sensitive to any warning sign—thinking a certain thought, my body feeling a certain way, the slightest thing I had associated with panic would send me straight into it.

A lot of the time I'd eventually vomit from the nausea and, for a little bit, I'd feel better, but I'd often work myself right back up again not long after. My parents had no idea what to do to help me.

My mom would do her best to stay awake with me, but, as I can now relate to as a parent myself, it's easy to drift off to sleep while lying next to your child, and that would also make me panic—I was all by myself, and my protector couldn't stay the vigil with me.

These episodes lasted for over a year, almost every night. I developed a level of self-awareness that was probably obscene for a seven-year-old.

I can't emphasize enough how alone these made me feel. I was trapped with myself, by myself, in my head. I analyzed the snot out of every thought I had, trying to understand what was going on with myself, trying to figure out how to make myself stop. I scrutinized every feeling, every thought, every action obsessively.

I developed an intense hatred of myself. I knew I was at fault for my own misery and, as much as I wanted to make it stop, I just couldn't.

I thought things about myself, about life, that no normal child thinks at that age—how could I be so weak, so pathetic, so worthless? Where was God? Why didn't he do anything? What good was he? What was the point of going on?

I just wanted the pain to stop. I wished I were dead quite a bit, just to make my mind shut up.

Then, the most innocent of conversations with my mom completely ended the attacks. I wished out loud one day that there was some kind of medication one could take to help with these sorts of things, and she told me there was.

Wait. What? There actually was medication that could help? I'd had no idea. I thought I had my own mind to save me, and that was it.

The knowledge by itself that I had a recourse available other than myself ended the attacks immediately. I didn't even need the medication—just knowing there was something I could do other than rely on myself freed me.

Coming out of my experience with panic in early childhood, I began to read voraciously. Somehow, I got it in my mind that I was going to read the entire Bible. So, without a plan in mind, I started in Genesis and just read. And read, and read, and read.

I made it through the Old Testament, then made it through the Gospels in the New Testament and stopped at the Acts of the Apostles (I think I just got tired). I didn't understand a large portion of what I read, and there's a decent bit of the Bible that isn't exactly child friendly, but it all wound its way between my ears.

It was near that time I discovered a love of science fiction and came across Isaac Asimov and his *Foundation* series, which I devoured. I'd enjoyed *Star Wars* movies as a smaller kid, but LucasFilm began publishing sequel novels at that time—I picked one up and became hooked, and that's where a deep love of *Star Wars* grew.

My mom's mother became seriously ill when I was in middle school. She and her husband lived south of Miami in a small community called Goulds. They stayed with us during Hurricane Andrew and, while their house survived, everything else on their property was completely wiped out.

My grandmother had been an alcoholic for decades, likely owing to her divorce with my grandfather in the mid-1940s, something she regretted for the rest of her life. After Andrew, she began to suffer from dementia and several other ailments.

My mom moved her up to live with us so she could take care of her and, as the dementia slowly ate away at her mind and her health continued to deteriorate, it took a severe toll on my mom and my family. The year or two she spent caring for my grandmother until she passed away in 1994 nearly brought her to her knees, and, at the ages of eleven and twelve, was a difficult time for me, too, as my mom was emotionally consumed with caring for her mom and dealing with her failing mind.

I became even more addicted to achievement. I determined I was going to graduate at the top of my class. I won a lot of academic contests and awards, and, unknown to me, I was thriving on this affirmation. I thought I could do anything.

My church recognized my gifts, too. The age of twelve is standard in the Methodist tradition I grew up in for a young person who has been baptized to join the church through a process called confirmation, so I did that, and—as a very emotionally-aware guy—I felt what Christians call a movement of the Holy Spirit within me.

As I started preparation for high school, a combination of factors began to mess with my childhood ambitions of becoming an archaeologist. First among those were the lingering effects of my panic episodes.

While in my best moments—when being lauded for my accomplishments—I felt like I could be anything, in my low moments when the echoes of panic and depression whispered in my head, I was petrified. I couldn't imagine going away to school and leaving my family, let alone pursuing a career that would have me traveling all over the world and job hunting from university to university. It also didn't match my growing ambitions, as I became more determined to become someone who people thought was important.

The echoes of fear likewise overruled the prospect of entering the Christian ministry in my mind. Into my mid-teenage years, as I became active in youth group and church leadership, I'd had opportunity to preach and write articles for the church newsletter and been encouraged to pursue the ministry. But how could I be a Methodist pastor, who was subject to moving all over the blasted state on a yearly basis?

I made my faith my own around the age of sixteen. I asked the deep questions of why in the world I believed what I did— why should I accept Christianity as true? I became attracted to apologetics, which is the intellectual defense of the Christian faith through history, science, and philosophy. At the time, despite my unresolved emotional traumas and pain with God, intellectually I was convinced.

Much to my friends' annoyance, I turned into Super Christian. I wanted to save the universe for God. I tried a few times to hold Bible studies to share my passion and awaken the same in my friends. I became a leader in high school in different Christian organizations. My church basically looked to me as the representative for my generation.

It was also at this time that my panic decided to start making an appearance again. Perhaps it was due in part to the hormones that started to flood my body because, boy oh boy, did I have it bad for the ladies. I'd write poems, songs, and letters to express myself. As these were the pre-cell phone days, I would exchange notes with girls in class on a regular basis.

But I was ridiculously shy and timid. And, good God, was I intense. A love-lost type of Romeo, living and dying on how my crushes felt about me. In hindsight, little wonder I dated very briefly in high school and was for the most part single.

That kind of brooding likely contributed to the melancholy and panic I began dealing with at the time, but I was able, with help, to get that back under what I thought was a small amount of control.

The academic awards, accolades, and peer affirmation piled up on top of each other from late middle school through the end of high school. I felt untouchable, in a way. Voted Most Likely to Succeed in middle school by my peers and Most Intelligent in high school. I graduated at the top of my class, co-valedictorian with a perfect GPA.

Everybody seemed to love me, affirm me, and kept telling me I could be anything in the world I wanted to be; there was nothing that could stop me. And I wanted to do something incredible with myself to show how important I was, something that would change the world somehow.

I had a full scholarship through college with anything I wanted to do at my fingertips, while the dragon birthed in a seven-year-old heart of emotional trauma, insecurity, self-hatred, panic, despair, and inadequacy slumbered beneath the surface. What could possibly go wrong?

3

COLORING OUR PERCEPTIONS

I 've come to learn the ways in which we've been hurt—our brokenness—changes how we see life. When I was younger, I thought that was crazy. Sure, I knew I had some biases, but there was no way my emotions could cloud my judgment that badly.

That changed several years ago.

I had been through a rough stretch. My choices and behavior had ruined my self-image and goals. I had a beautiful baby girl, but my relationship with her mother had fallen apart. To top it off, I lost my job.

I'd reached a rock-bottom moment but was on the mend. I'd started to know in my heart what had only made it to my head, that I had real problems. Good friends and a good community were slowly helping to heal some of my wounds.

But I was having some minor issues with the church I'd started attending. It was trivial stuff. I thought the King James-language liturgy and the fancy vestments worn by the priests were out-of-date and distracting, which hurt the effectiveness of the church's witness. It was a language too hard for the average person to understand and an attire too alien for a postmodern culture.

I found myself one night at a Bible study with a close group of friends. I don't remember what we were discussing or how the topic came up, but eventually the conversation drifted to what the nature of Christ's suffering on the cross was about. I shared that I thought in a mysterious way Christ took on the weight of every sin every human being would ever commit, that he felt every pain. A few of my friends disagreed.

I remember becoming more agitated as the conversation went on. I finally said, "No, God has to have experienced all that on the cross. Because if he doesn't know my pain personally, then [expletive] him. What kind of God would that be? No, [expletive] him if he can't relate to me."

I clearly remember saying that, and I remember the rawness of it and saying it with full conviction, without a second thought. I don't so much look back in horror at it now (for those concerned, I repented)—I look back trying to remember what emotions I was tapping in to. Because as the years have gone by, I continued to heal, and several things have changed.

I now know I reacted the way I did because I saw it as an attack on a fragile thread I was holding on to, which was the only way I could see God feeling what I'd just gone through in my life. I've realized the issues I was having over liturgy and vestments were tied into this pain—they spoke to me of God being far away when I wanted him right here in my world experiencing my hurt. Going all "thee, thou, beseech" on me while looking like someone from 1,500 years ago made God feel more distant.

What's interesting is this: there is some legitimacy to all those points. They aren't worthless or without insight. But. They weren't the real issue, were they?

And as the real issue began to be more fully addressed—as I continued to let go of pain and hold on to the truth that God is a God who is with us—my ideological arguments carried less urgency, and I began to appreciate the bigger picture: God is intimately with us, but at the same time he is holy and set apart.

Jesus may not know from experience what it's like to have a romantic relationship implode, but he's in tune with a deeper understanding of pain and suffering than I will ever be.

Damage and brokenness impact how we see the world. And you and I surely aren't self-aware enough to recognize at all times how it's happening in ourselves. We need friends—community—to help us out with our blind spots. We need wisdom in handling our thoughts and ideas, and humility to empathize with others and embrace the possibility we might actually be wrong about some things.

ANGER IS COMMONLY ASSOCIATED with pain and trauma, but any emotion can cloud our vision and distort the way we see reality. There's a quote attributed to English theologian Thomas Cranmer I find very profound and relevant: "What the heart desires, the will chooses, and the mind justifies."

Take lust as an example. My own experience as a former hormonally-imbalanced teenage boy who wanted to find a way for his sex drive to be satisfied despite his Christian morals is a good case study.

With the advantages brought from age, learning, and life experience, I now have a better grasp of the reasons why the orthodox Christian conviction is that sex is intended for marriage. Very briefly, it's because humans imitate God; God is Trinity and in constant relationship within the three persons; it is as male and female together that God formed humanity in his image; therefore the way for humans to evoke God in sexuality is for the male plus female image to enjoy each other within the same kind of committed relationship the Trinity has within the Godhead.

But as a teenager, all I knew was there were verses in Scripture forbidding being promiscuous. Little horn dog that I was, though, what my heart desired didn't take too much massaging of the Biblical text for my will to choose to let my mind justify it away. After all, I reasoned, wasn't it written to a culture with different morals? People who thought it should still apply today were missing the point that the references against pre-marital sex were written in a letter addressed to a specific group of people at a particular time with unique circumstances, right? So, that doesn't apply to me.

My beliefs were clearly being manipulated by other motivations and not the pursuit of truth for truth's sake.

LET'S TRY A QUICK EXERCISE. Take a moment and try to self-assess the ways you think and act as best you can. Do anger or lust ever effect you? Do you get so upset over some issues that you can't even consider alternatives? Or do you think you've worked through all your hang-ups, so you're no longer biased?

The end of modernism (the era of Western culture preceding, as the name suggests, postmodernism) has taught us at least one valuable lesson: whether it's anger, lust, joy, sorrow, peace, restlessness, apathy, or any other of the host of emotions and mindsets out there, at some level we are all biased. Because people are the creators of knowledge and ideas, there is no such thing as an idea existing independent of some sort of bias(es).

There is also no such thing as a completely objective observer because a person, by definition, sees things subjectively. Surely things exist outside subjective perception, but for a human to process something, it must go through an interpretive machine: our minds.

The best we can do is try to understand how our perceptions are being influenced and then try to compensate for those influences.

For myself, in addition to experiencing anger, I can be melancholy, so recognizing that one of my temptations is to look at life in a glass-half-empty kind of way is important if I want to try to view life as realistically as I can. I also need my friends to correct me when I don't realize I'm being especially biased.

N.T. Wright addresses this well in a lecture titled *What's the Problem with Jesus?* given at the C.S. Lewis Institute in January 2002:

What about the popular religious culture of our day? . . . there's all sorts of things about the voyage of religious self-discovery . . . the discovery of "who I really am." You know, "For half of my life I thought I was this sort of person and now I'm discovering the deep truth about who I really am inside." . . . Jesus is often called in at this point so that discovering Jesus is sort of a symbol of discovering "who I really am," and Jesus becomes the patron saint of the voyage of self-discovery . . .

My friend Marcus Borg is in print telling his own story this way. He grew up in a little Midwest town in a very conservative Lutheran church, [he was] taught you had to believe the following nineteen things and then you'd be justified by faith and you'd go to heaven, and you had to behave in certain ways, etc., etc. Then you [sic] grew up and went to seminary and discovered there was a wider world out there at the same time he discovered source criticism of the Gospels and he hasn't looked back.

And Marcus went through a classic pattern of losing his faith and rediscovering it . . . It's the story that so many Americans have gone through. And it's then a way of rediscovering some sort of faith which isn't like that faith you had when you were a kid. And Marcus and that whole generation, the one thing they don't want is to go back to that narrow little world they grew up in. And so, they will find anything in the scholarly constructs that they can to prevent them from going back there. They will find more exciting ways of being a Christian, supposedly.

In fact, this sustains, I believe, a totally illegitimate process of doing history. It conveniently ignores all the sharp edges of Christianity, and actually, though it appears to underwrite a voyage of self-discovery in which the old rules don't apply, it may well only be hearing the echo of its own voice rather than actually doing anything serious historically.

PSYCHOLOGICALLY SPEAKING, WHAT WE perceive to be real is, for our minds, real. It's unfortunate if we believe we can walk through traffic without getting hit by a car, but that is where actual reality can uncomfortably confront our sometimes-misguided mental reality.

I'm at a point in my Christian faith where I can relate to St. Augustine's classic prayer from his *Confessions*: "Our hearts are restless, O God, until they find rest in Thee." I've been floundering there for a while, trying to find this rest.

I've been told on good authority that one of my stumbling blocks is a belief deep within my heart that God isn't actually good. And supposedly when I receive more evidence of his goodness in my life, I will be able to accept this at a deeper level.

The thing is, I think that evidence has been there all along, but it's just not clicking with my heart. I'm just not very grateful. I'm not sure why.

I guess a good question is: should I be grateful? I actually think I should be. But I'm not. I've done the thing where you make a list of all the stuff you ought to be grateful for in life, and it is a humbling experience that highlights the many things I'm prone to shove out of my conscious mind and take for granted. But it hasn't changed my attitude.

Bertrand Russell, an English philosopher who wrote a lot about his atheism, was once asked what he would say to God upon death if it is found out that he is real. As quoted in *An Introduction to the Philosophy of Religion* by Michael J. Murray and Michael C. Rea, he said he would reply, "Not enough evidence, God! Not enough evidence!"

Which begs the same question regarding my gratefulness— what in the world would constitute *enough*? We can have an idea in our minds of what that would be, but if we are prone to disbelief, it's likely—given time—that we will push the line that defines "enough" further out once we've crossed it.

So, about gratefulness and my perception. The uncomfortable thought I'm having is . . . maybe it's time I just chose it. Maybe when something good happens, no matter how small, I should make myself express gratitude to God. Even though I think that's a stupid thing to do. Even though I don't want to.

And I think I can let myself still complain when bad things happen. I just need to balance it with the proper attention due the good things. The things that are good that are so easy to ignore: waking up every day, taking another breath, having another heart beat, seeing my daughter, feeling the sun on my skin.

Maybe that's the way to get my mind where it ought to be.

4

WHY WE THINK THIS WAY

W hy am I the way I am? What makes you, well, you? We've discussed how genetics and environment (nature and nurture) are two primary influences. Taken together, we're made up of genes and experiences that are deeply interconnected, with genetics affecting our perception of our experiences and experiences altering the structure of our genes. Our will, our heart's desires, flow from this spring.

We're usually able to recognize desires within ourselves that are healthy and unhealthy. On basic points, we tend to agree: anger is damaging when left unaddressed; bitterness eats away at us; real love is healing and empowering.

If we're interested in being happy and healthy, we will—with help—begin to confront the demons that are eating away at us from the inside. That's very hard and intimidating, but the alternative is to live in a state of bare existence. Sometimes existing is all we're able to do for a season, but that's a really depressing end goal for our lives.

Eventually the things we use to distract ourselves so we don't have to deal with our problems will be gone. If we dive into the reasons why we crave these distractions, if we begin to heal from our damage, we begin to live with more joy.

And the reasons we should consider doing this aren't just self-ish. If we care about the people we are close to, we will confront our darkness for their sake, because when we're honest with ourselves, we know our damage hurts those we love.

STARTING IN ADOLESCENCE, our chosen group of loved ones often have the strongest influence on what we choose to believe about life. Our friends and the communities we choose to associate with can begin to control how we identify ourselves without us realizing it.

We're all motivated to think and act in the ways we do in order to gain the approval of people or groups of people whose opinions we value. We seek validation, and likely one of the first forms of validation we received came from parental figures whom reinforced specific thoughts and behaviors.

As we mature from childhood into adulthood, we begin to craft our own self-perception. Often this includes rejecting certain parts of our parental figures' thought and action and selecting other role models, usually from our peers.

But we don't always choose our friends or the groups we associate with. Most of the time we gravitate toward anyone who provides companionship, friendship, or love. And being accepted or respected by these people then becomes really important to us because we both like them and fear we might not find other people who will accept us.

Just as crucially, we close off our minds from groups we think are opposed to our own group, which both fosters prejudice and limits our point of view (this is especially obvious today in the tribalism of our hyper-partisan, polarized politics).

A fictitious example to demonstrate the point: why would I as a libertarian who believes government is the cause of society's problems even begin to imagine why a socialist thinks having a very involved government is better? What if I actually started to find the socialist's ideas compelling? What would my friends think? What would I think about myself? The fear of possibly changing my opinion and therefore being ostracized from my chosen community closes off my mind from the possibility of learning something new and important.

All of us seek the respect and affirmation of certain people and to some extent allow our thoughts and behaviors to be determined by whomever those people are. The best we can do is recognize this and realize that if we lose our community just because our opinions or beliefs change, then that community didn't truly love and accept us to begin with.

SPEAKING OF OUR THOUGHTS: what does it mean to know something? Most folks would probably point to the scientific method as the best path to knowledge. If you can test it and demonstrate it, the thinking goes, you know it more certainly than anything else.

But is scientific knowledge really the best kind? Why do we think it is? What other kinds of knowledge are there?

Seventeenth-century French philosopher Rene Descartes popularized the idea that certainty—knowing something without any room for doubt—is the most ideal kind of knowledge. Modern science quickly became popular in part because the scientific method includes a step for repeatability, and the more often something can be verified by repeating it, the more certain we feel it is.

Science has shown itself to be effective in explaining several aspects of our physical reality, and over the last few hundred years, advances in scientific knowledge have directly led to more power and more wealth.

To the person who has invested large portions of his or her life to science, the tendency is to associate science with the top of a kind of knowledge hierarchy. But I don't think the way we live our everyday lives suggests that most of us, in practice, treat science as our most important kind of knowledge.

For example, I know I love my daughter, and I order most of my life around this knowledge. And love is not scientific. While the emotions associated with love can be explained by science, I don't use the scientific method to know I love someone.

Likewise, the way we know other people in relationships and the ways we learn how to perform jobs and develop skills are not scientific. I know my family and my friends not just by the facts I know about them and behaviors I observe, but more intimately through some mysterious way in which I begin to know the essence of who they are. I learned how to play guitar and sense timing in music not by observing where my fingers naturally moved or what my ear heard, but through training my fingers and ears through repetition that developed an unquantifiable skill.

None of this is meant to belittle science, but simply to make clear that the kinds of knowledge we use in everyday life aren't usually scientific. We need to realize the meanings we give to facts don't come from some neutral place, but from a mesh of motivations.

There is no such thing as pure objectivity, and Descartes' dream of certainty—knowledge without any doubt—is impossible, because doubt isn't connected to knowledge, but instead comes out of our biases and beliefs. One can choose to doubt anything. Something we think is obvious isn't necessarily obvious to everyone else.

At our most basic levels, we are all operating on faith. We don't typically recognize the faith we use every day as faith, though. But when you really begin to peer into the depths of what is certain, you realize just how dependent we are on faith for everything.

I ACTUALLY LOVE SCIENCE.

In middle school I became fascinated with time travel. I wrote a series of research papers over four years that began with time travel as the premise, but ended with my best efforts as a fourteen-year-old in analyzing the most recent quantum physics theories about the natures of time, space, and reality.

In high school, I became interested in Evolutionary Theory, pouring over the details of natural selection, species adaptation, and the commonalities shared at the genetic level across known life.

I fell in love with science fiction, particularly the sub-genre called hard science fiction, which incorporates scientific theory into fiction to imagine possible future worlds.

I kept noticing a tendency reappearing across what I read, though, and it was very similar to something I'd noted while growing up in a Protestant Christian environment in the rural American South during the 1990s: many scientists seemed motivated to turn the interpretation of their findings into a religion, while the religious seemed motivated to redefine science.

You know the story, I'm sure, and I have no interest in re-hashing it. Suffice to say, in particular regarding evolution, many scientists wanted to use the field for the non-scientific purpose of debunking God's existence, while many religious people wanted to discredit much of accepted science to defend God.

Here's the deal: people—regardless of who we are, what we believe, or how we think—rely on interpretation to create meaning for our experiences. Like the classic cliché of the glass with water at the midpoint—is it half-empty or half-full? The fact is the glass is at half-capacity. Interpretation is how we answer the question, "What does that fact mean?"

Everybody interprets and creates meaning. Even if you conclude life itself has no meaning, that in itself acts as your meaning: your metanarrative, to revisit that postmodern term.

You're likely to interpret new experiences to fit within the story you believe about life. And you'll tend to ignore or reinterpret whatever would contradict your metanarrative. Everyone does this to some extent.

For whatever reason, we humans are meaning makers.

Science is a process of acquiring knowledge about physical reality through an objective, structured method. But this kind of pure science only exists hypothetically, because total objectivity—observing something without any bias—is impossible.

Some might disagree at first, because an argument can be made stating, "There's nothing biased about witnessing 'A' combine with 'B' to produce 'C,'" and that's true enough. But bias is still in the bigger picture, because the reason for observing "A, B, C" came because a scientist wanted to know something specific, had some form of vested interest in the outcome of the observation (be it grant money, prestige, tenure, or peer respect), and chose to observe "A, B, C" instead of observing "X, Y, Z."

What we too often hear from scientists are their interpretations and personal metanarratives masquerading as science, like an evolutionary scientist spouting that science disproves God's existence.

On the other hand, what we too often see from Christians is an attempt to co-opt science to serve a predetermined conclusion, like a young-earth creationist looking for any kind of data to support his or her beliefs.

Both approaches abuse what science is. Science is a way of knowledge, and it's powerful, but it's not the only way.

It's within the last 300 years, though, that modern science has demonstrated itself to be more tangibly powerful than any other form of knowledge. The drastic advances of technology and the increase in mastery over much of nature give science what appears to be the ultimate trump card: airplanes, rockets, medicine, computers, smart phones, tablets—faster, smarter, more efficient, better.

In the realm of human knowledge, science is Goliath. That puts a person who would appear to disagree with something identified as scientific in a precarious position.

But that brings us back to philosophy in order to ask what it truly means to disagree with science. Really, it isn't usually people who disagree with science itself (though some exceptions are notable, including those who reject climate change and that the Earth is round); it's people who disagree with other people claiming to speak for science but actually sharing their interpretations and metanarratives.

For example, some claim science states God isn't real because life evolved from non-life, so God doesn't exist. No, scientists are still trying to figure out how life likely began but are fairly confident life has evolved into different forms over millions of years. Science says nothing about what that means. People do.

Or, some claim science states there had to have been some sort of creator because the universe began with a Big Bang—nothing physical exists, then, bang, energy and matter. No, scientists currently accept the physical universe did indeed begin with an explosion resulting from a singularity, but because scientific law applies only to nature as we can observe and test it, we can't know what the rules outside our universe are (or if there even are any). Science says nothing about what that means. People do.

The battle most people have is not with science itself, it's with the people who want to make science do what it can't do—provide meaning—or who don't separate their interpretations of scientific results from the results themselves.

So, by all means, let's have our debates about what scientific findings and theories mean, but let's not try to bludgeon each other as if any of us speaks with the authority of science. And let's understand that debating the meaning of anything ultimately leads us to philosophy.

IF YOU'RE INTERESTED IN finding out if something is true—if your perception is accurate; if you're seeing things as they really are as best you can—then you need some healing in your life.

I have some difficult news for you that needs to be stated clearly: you're an emotionally broken person. It's inevitable that you're carrying around all sorts of hurts within you from childhood, adolescence, young adulthood, and adulthood, even if you've gone through professional counseling and made a lot of progress.

Even then, because life continues to happen and nothing we seem to do as humans is ever 100 percent effective, it's likely that any healing process you've gone through hasn't been complete.

That's not a popular thing to say in our culture, which relies on the belief we are self-made and are our own people. Sad to say, though, this just isn't true. We are in large part the product of our life experiences.

Only to the extent we have begun to heal from how we've been hurt are we in any way free from our past. Otherwise we're subconsciously guided like marionettes by how we've internalized our wounds.

Don't believe me? I hate to use this example because it's singling out a particular group of people, but in my observation it's one of the most obvious examples: look at any of the literature coming from the movement that calls itself the "new atheists," with writers such as Richard Dawkins and Christopher Hitchens. Almost without fail, anger and resentment flow off the pages these folks write, lambasting God, religions, and those who believe in said religions.

One thing I respect about these authors is at least they admit they're driven to their beliefs because they don't want God to exist—they can't bring themselves to believe in a universe where God is real because they don't want to.

Almost without exception, these folks are very intelligent. And though I do think there are some flaws in their logic and reasoning, regardless, here's the thing: when the tone of what they write is angry, resentful, and judgmental, and they honestly admit they're driven to their beliefs because they don't want to believe in the alternative, how impartially are they viewing reality?

Sounds to me like an awful lot of hurt that hasn't been dealt with coming out and coloring their perspectives. But fair is fair: as I've even said about myself, a lot of belief in God comes down to people ultimately wanting to believe.

What can we do? Is there such a thing as a correct desire that leads one to truth, or is reality completely relative to the observer? At the end of the day, I'm not sure there's an intellectual answer to satisfy those questions. I can address them from my point of view, but you'd have to come to trust it over and against other points of view.

Short of a definitive argument, you have to take a look at the kind of people who are presenting points of view—are they in the process of healing from the hurts of life, or are they embracing in various forms a path of anger, resentment, and ultimately self-destruction?

WHAT DOES IT MEAN to worship? The root of the word is "worth," so the most basic meaning is to assign worth to something. We all think some ideal, person, or thing has a kind of ultimate worth—it's a basic human characteristic to be a worshiper.

When we worship something, we elevate its importance. A thing in itself can be good, bad, or neutral, but when we worship it (invest ultimate importance in it), we magnify whatever qualities it possesses.

I think we worship the ideal of freedom as a kind of civil religion in America. Whether one is an atheist, Christian, Buddhist, Muslim, Hindu, Democrat, Republican, Communist, Socialist, whatever—freedom permeates every religion, every worldview, every philosophy, every mindset of our culture and our heritage.

Perhaps more broadly we worship our rights as humans, but first and foremost among those rights is a particular idea of freedom. "Don't tread on me." "No taxation without representation." "Give me liberty or give me death." We want our speech to be free, our religion to be free, our markets to be free, our right to weaponry to be free, our sexuality to be free, our morality to be free, our press to be free.

And I think this "Gospel of Freedom" is destroying us as individuals and as a society.

That doesn't mean I think freedom is bad—I think it's incredibly important. Vital. But it isn't supposed to be an object of worship, and when it's treated like one, it (like all things that weren't meant to be worshiped) has its limitations distorted and intensified.

There is more than one way to understand what freedom is. I think it's best understood as a kind of acceptance rather than the ability to choose. True freedom doesn't reside in having unlimited choices, but rather in accepting reality and what our identity is.

Are we free when we understand and embrace who we truly are as people, or when we feed ourselves with an endless supply of options and choices?

We've allowed our culture to convince us that freedom to make any choices we want is the only actual kind of freedom there is, and that is a lie. Our cultural worship of this form of freedom has hijacked our understanding of human identity and our ability to engage in successful and meaningful dialogue with those we fundamentally disagree with, and it has led us down a path of rampant consumerism and exploitation.

This concept of freedom is a wolf in sheep's clothing. It's a tyrant keeping us separated from real freedom and clouding our minds so we can't clearly see who we as humans truly are.

CLIMAX

It's been several months' worth of cleaning, and I'm still at it: this tombstone is stubborn. Decades and decades of dirt, soil, moss, and mold have stained it to the point that I'm not sure what its natural color is.

I've bought gallons of biological cleaning solution to restore it without causing damage bleach or other chemicals would, but the tradeoff is in elbow grease and time.

I've scrubbed and poured cleaner on both broken pieces and the footer a number of times, then left them outside at my parents' Florida home for the elements to assist the process. It's become a ritual when I visit my folks, my regular practice to go scrub an old stone for about an hour in the sun.

Whether it will prove fruitful enough for it to be restored remains to be seen. Some journeys have to be taken without knowing what the destination will be.

TURNS OUT ONE OF the first things that can go wrong after leaving high school is not having a clue what you want to do in college. Since I'd written off history, I settled on my other early love, writing, and majored in journalism. I didn't anticipate a career in journalism itself, per se, but maybe writing that elusive Great American Novel? Yeah, that could match my ambitions.

Another thing that can go wrong is an emotional crisis of identity in an immature heart. As I've said, I found love for the first time during the summer after graduating high school, and, goodness, I fell hard.

There was a large gulf between my intellectual and emotional maturity, so I was full throttle from day one in a relationship. So happens that, no matter what one's good intentions may be, if you play around with enough fire, you're going to get burned, so it came as a shock to my system when my Christian morality collapsed in the face of my teenage sex drive.

When the relationship ended, I was a basket case. Who I thought I was as a Christian was a mess. Who I thought I'd be for the woman I'd end up marrying was down the tubes. I didn't think my heart was capable of coming back together. In some ways, it was the most painful breakup I've had because of how unprepared my heart was.

The early years of college were a breeze in the classroom. I lucked into an internship with the University of Florida's student newspaper, *The Independent Florida Alligator*, and I hated every minute of it. I had to relearn how to write for journalism, and it's the opposite of creative writing. Journalism is crisp, to the point. Make use of as few words as possible. Pertinent information summarized up front, supporting details in the body, no real conclusion at the end.

But I learned to do it, and I became a better writer because of it. And I affirmed that a career in journalism was not for me, at least not one in a fast-paced, cut-throat environment. So I decided to change majors within the College of Journalism to public relations—I justified to myself that learning to deal with the public at large and influence opinions could be useful as I attempted to make a mark on society.

In my personal life, I became more interested in music. I'd picked up a guitar at nineteen and started teaching myself to play. I took a class at the local community college, and a new friend who started attending my church was an excellent musician who was happy to teach me more. He was interested in forming a band that could perform at special church functions for fun.

Swell idea, I thought, and since he already played the guitar, I switched to bass. We put together a little band and, as always happens within a church whenever someone shows competence and a willingness to do something, we found ourselves thrust into work within the space of about a year, leading worship at one of two Sunday services.

My spiritual life was growing, but not in the ways I truly needed. I'd finally finished reading through the Bible and reread it because it's not like a novel you read once and you're done with it. It's something you saturate yourself with and let sink into your marrow.

I'd had some spiritual experiences with God and felt his presence as I prayed, but I didn't realize that I needed him to heal the wounds my heart had picked up as a seven-year-old and then added to throughout my life. Self-hatred, insecurity, inadequacy, and—most of all—fear were still inside me, just dormant most of the time.

Out of dread of prodding them awake, I let them lie. On good days, I convinced myself they weren't really there like they once were. I knew a heck of a lot in my head about God and who he was and how one ought to be a Christian, but he hadn't healed my heart.

A year ticked by and I found myself at age twenty doing alright in school and being active in my church but otherwise kind of feeling uninspired about life, unsure how public relations was going to help me be a world changer like I'd hoped it would.

Then a mentor and friend of mine at my church decided to run for office as a circuit judge. I offered to help him out, so I analyzed some voter data and organized some sign-waving events. Circuit judge races are non-partisan, but he was a registered Republican, so we received some assistance from local Republican groups, especially the UF College Republicans, where I was introduced to and befriended their leader.

And, wouldn't you know it, my friend pulled off an upset and won the race. I enjoyed political campaigning; it was rather thrilling and felt important.

My church hired a new youth director around that time, and she became a part of the worship team I was in. We hit it off pretty well, and soon she suggested that I consider helping out as an assistant with the youth: I knew a lot about God, and I was young enough to relate. So I did that for a little less than a year and had fun, establishing good relationships with the kids and overall feeling like I was doing something to advance the church.

Not long after I turned twenty-one, as happens too frequently in smaller churches, a kerfuffle with the youth director occurred over something minor that got blown out of proportion and resulted in her stepping down. The other helpers wanted no part of leadership, so interim duties fell to me by default.

I found myself filling in as the youth director while helping lead a worship team and going to school full time. I was on the Staff-Parrish Relations Committee, which in the United Methodist Church is in charge of hiring and firing, so I sat in on the interviews to fill the position.

My mentor the circuit judge was the head of this committee and, after about the fourth unsuccessful interview, in exasperation asked me why I didn't just take the job since I'd been filling in so well. I prayed about it and surprisingly felt affirmed in the decision, so I accepted.

I read a ton of books on how to lead a youth ministry and, on the surface, things went well. The kids seemed engaged, I put together lessons geared toward familiarizing them more with Scripture and knowledge about Jesus, and I invested my time in their lives. The group slowly grew, and things were going swimmingly everywhere except in my heart and mind.

I hit a road block in college. I somehow managed to box myself in to needing six classes to finish my undergraduate degree, but each of those was a prerequisite for the other, so I was looking at two more years to finish a four-year degree I'd already invested four years in.

A good friend of mine suggested I look at switching majors to political science just to complete my degree, something he'd recently done. When I compared the classes I'd taken with the degree requirements, sure enough, the history and philosophy courses I'd taken as electives made a degree realistic in about a year. And, I reasoned, maybe I could go to law school afterward and pursue a political career, and that would be how I impacted the world.

The year 2004 rolled around and with it a presidential election, and the former College Republican friend I'd made during the circuit judge campaign had become head of the county Republican Party. I parlayed that relationship into a credited internship to work on the Bush-Cheney reelection campaign, and my emphasis within my political science major became political campaigning.

Meanwhile, I'd been a year into being a full-time youth director, and it was taking a toll. I was spent. I'd been devouring the Bible to come up with lessons and, as one becomes more familiar with Scripture, one tends to start asking some serious questions. Why is my experience of God so boring and bland? Why doesn't God speak to me like he did to so many others? Why am I lonely and emotionally vulnerable when I'm doing God's work?

I was running on empty spiritually. Where was the God who was so active in Scripture to help give me energy to do his ministry? Constantly pouring myself out in service to others without knowing how to receive more love and affirmation from God drained me.

Church worship began to feel dead to me, like a meeting of a Rotary Club instead of something alive and interactive with God. I was frustrated with my life. I was burnt out, stressed, directionless, and lonely.

That carried on for about another year while I kept asking God for help and, by all appearances, he remained silent. So, I inadvertently sabotaged myself. I took my happiness into my own hands, resigned as youth director, and entered into a romantic relationship I had no business being in.

I graduated from college in December 2005 and had absolutely no idea what to do with myself. I'd started looking for life in church outside my own tradition, wondering if there were any Christians who had some sort of more spiritual connection with

God that weren't over-the-top like I thought some charismatics were.

In 2006, my acquaintance, the head of the county Republican Party, decided to run for an open state senate seat. I reached out to him to ask if he needed help, and, sure enough, I became a de facto kind of campaign manager during the primary. Now, finally, I thought, something could actually come of my life, and I could redirect my rising self-hatred regarding how much I'd failed my potential—my guy wins the senate seat, I become a legislative aid in Tallahassee, bam, rising political career where I can really make a difference in people's lives.

He did a lot better than he should have in the primary, but he lost to the former county sheriff, who enjoyed a big advantage in name recognition and fundraising. And in the process, I became disgusted with American politics and how sketchy a lot of it seemed to me.

So, my life was listless. Then 2007 came around and, wham, my girlfriend was pregnant. Scandalously so given my former stature in church. Old panic, self-hatred, and insecurity reemerged in force: what a freaking wreck I was, a failure, a fraud I told myself over and over.

I tried to make things as right as I could and marry her, but she wasn't ready. So, pending fatherhood, I knew I had to get a better job than the ones I'd had so far, no matter what it was.

I lucked out and got a job at a construction engineering firm, where I made one of the best friends I've ever had. He was brilliant and a devout Christian who had faced some of the same questions and crises I was currently going through in my faith, and he belonged to a church with a bunch of like-minded guys I was blessed to meet. I'd never met a group like them, people I could relate to with my questions and crises.

By 2008, my daughter was born and I was promoted at my job. Things were looking up.

Then the bottom fell out.

The recession hit the construction industry, and I was laid off out of the blue. The turmoil my fiancé and I had been through over the past three-plus years finally became too much for her, and she left me. I could no longer go through the motions of attending my family's church where I felt spiritually dead.

The dragon of panic, fear, insecurity, rage, and inadequacy fully awoke from its slumber in my heart and inflamed like never before. My self-perception, my faith, everything I held onto went up in flames as I fell apart.

PRAYER OF REPENTANCE—TO KNOW GOD TRULY

Father, though we have sinned against you and are not worthy, we humbly beg you to deliver us from ourselves.

We have made you, your son, and your spirit in our image and likeness and not sought to know who you truly are.

We have prophesied in your name and in your name driven out demons and performed many miracles, but we did not know you.

We repent of the numerous idols we have worshiped instead of you: ourselves; our desires; our beliefs; our rights; our freedoms; our prejudices; our nation; power; money; sex; fame; family.

We have blasphemed your name by using it to support our own agendas while claiming they were yours.

We have not loved our neighbor as ourselves.

We have not followed Jesus' example of leading others through self-sacrifice and service, but have instead sought to lead others by Caesar's example through force and coercion.

Forgive us for our pride, presumption, and arrogance, both volitional and subconscious.

Father, give us the desire and the ability to seek you for your glory and not our own.

Help us to know your heart and your character, to worship and serve you in spirit and in truth.

Grant us discerning, pure, and humble hearts in order to mold us into the true likeness of your son.

May we serve you truly, Father, and know you more fully from this day on.

In the name of Jesus Christ, our only mediator and advocate, we ask these things. Amen.

5

STARTING TO UNDERSTAND LOVE AND WHO WE ARE

We tend to let our emotions and biases skew our perceptions. Perhaps more than with anything else, this is especially true when it comes to love.

How we define what love is influences every other idea we have regarding our interactions with people. You'll be hard-pressed to find anyone who doesn't believe there is a thing called love that is central to human life. But what in the world is it?

There are a lot of problems surrounding the term "love" because we use it to define a number of different things: infatuation, lust, happiness, passion, desire. Let's try to break it down and see if we can agree on its core.

The first thing that comes to mind when we talk about love is feelings. Our society often uses feelings alone to define love—if I love you it's because you make me feel a certain way, so love must be a feeling (apologies to Boston's "More Than A Feeling").

For many people, that's probably all love is. That's why the divorce rate is so high—if love is a feeling, when I stop feeling a certain way about you, it must mean I don't love you anymore.

While anyone who has a decent amount of life experience under-stands feelings are fickle and can change sporadically, nonetheless many of us would probably consider ending a marriage if our feel-ings were acting strange.

Maybe that is indeed all love is. Maybe it's only an emotion. But that's a very recent idea and not how love has historically been understood.

Within the Christian story, love is a principle—a decision of the will. We still give this understanding of love lip service in wed-ding vows. But when the rubber hits the road and feelings change, our actions carry out what we deeply believe.

As a society our actions state that we think love is a feeling, and marriage is contingent on that transitory feeling. Just as with fleeting emotions, just as with the consumerism that is imbedded in our subconscious, love becomes another thing to be picked up or discarded according to our whims, because we think it's only about one person: me. Love becomes another commodity.

No, this is not love. True love comes down to two principles: commitment and sacrifice. Yes, emotions are connected with love. It'd be odd if we never had positive feelings for someone we love. But they aren't necessary nor to be expected constantly. Love is an oath I take, implicitly or explicitly, and it looks different depending on the context.

I make it a priority to tell my daughter "I love you" a lot, and I tell her what that means so the love has a definition attached to it. It means I will always be available to help her; I will care about her no matter what; and I will care about her health, well-being, and life more than I do my own. The commitment is that will never change, and the sacrifice is that I will take away from myself—even when it hurts—to give to her.

The level of commitment and sacrifice will differ depending on the relationship, but they are foundational to all forms of love. If that's true, we should expect love to hurt. It won't be easy. It's work, hard work. The hardest and most important work in our lives.

WHEN IT COMES TO being in love, some of us are lucky. We have a high school sweetheart, fall madly in love, and get married and stay married for sixty years. For others of us, it doesn't quite work out that way.

Be it the inability to find anyone to love us, a lack of faithfulness by ourselves or our partner, abuse, neglect, or death, we find our hearts shattered, broken, stretched, hardened. When my first relationship after high school ended, I wasn't sure my heart would ever recover. It took a long time; years, in fact, because I was young, immature, and didn't know how to foster healing.

But it did heal. And I fell in love again about five years later. That relationship lasted a lot longer, but it, too, ended in heartbreak and confusion. The pain in some ways wasn't as intense the second time around, but in other ways it was worse.

So, what is the heart capable of? How can it love multiple people across a lifetime?

When my heart is hurting, I think a good bit about widows and widowers who remarry, people who have been in love with someone and then tragically lost them only to (eventually) love someone else enough to marry them. Does that mean they suddenly no longer love their previous spouse? No, I don't think that's true at all. It means they've learned the truth that the heart is capable of holding a lot of love.

We know this is true when we think of our children. Those of us with more than one kid know that our hearts expand with the birth of each one in ways we may have not thought possible, increasing our ability to love. We find more room to love more people.

Because love is a commitment, a selfless depth of care for another person, in theory there's no limit to the number of people we can love, and in fact the Christian affirmation is that we are, genuinely, to love everyone.

Every person I've been in love with I've loved uniquely, because each person is different. They hold their own place in my heart. Healing occurs in stages as my heart learns to let them go, but, as in the case of widowhood, the terms of letting go can be different depending on how a relationship ends.

First and foremost, healing takes time. Time, time, time. It also takes intentionality. You aren't just going to heal by letting time pass. And it takes patience and perseverance.

Healing occurs in layers. Agonizing, frustrating layers. The depth of pain and trauma we've been through can cut through us deeply. As we heal from one aspect of it, a layer is removed like an onion, and we find yet another layer of pain lying underneath.

I think the first step in healing is forgiveness. Unfortunately, many of us don't understand what real forgiveness is. To forgive someone doesn't mean we completely ignore what they've done to us.

Forgiveness is acknowledging the pain and the evil that took place and confronting it. It's saying to someone (even if not to that person's face) what they did was wrong; it hurt; it was not right; but I choose to not hold it against you in my heart anymore.

The heart can't truly heal unless we forgive. It will lug around our pain and trauma indefinitely otherwise. Honestly, I think forgiveness is called for even with death. If we lose a spouse or loved one to death, part of us has to forgive them for dying—when someone dies, they leave us, and we aren't always ready for them to go.

The second step in healing is letting go. It's acknowledging the relationship is over, be it because of death, abuse, or cheating. Just like forgiving, this can be hard. It involves mourning the death of something, even if that something is the kind of person or relationship we loved.

Twice when my heart was broken, the other person helped me let go by moving on to a new relationship—it was obvious to me they were, in fact, done with me. It hurt a lot. But it made the process of letting go faster and easier.

Despite that, it still took years for my heart to recover fully, and the word "fully" may be a bit of a misnomer—my heart still carries feelings for both those women who meant a lot to me at different points in my life.

That's just the way the heart is. In a sense, I don't think feelings ever truly, completely die. They just heal to the point that they aren't weights around our souls, holding us back from experiencing more love in life.

Widows and widowers who remarry have learned the lesson that the heart is capable of holding love for multiple people in healthy ways. They accept that one love is gone, though that doesn't mean their heart has stopped loving them—it means they've learned another person can have his or her own place in their heart, too.

Once we choose to love someone, the feeling of falling in love will eventually come. That's been a hard one for me to understand and accept. And even if hypothetically that feeling never does come, so what? That kind of infatuation isn't love itself. But it comes through trust. Deeper levels of love result in building trust, which takes time. Deep, deep trust, especially for people who have been wounded, takes a long time to establish, and that's OK.

That's why the commitment aspect of love is so important. If you love someone, you're choosing to stick around, come what may. You're going to give the effort, time, and patience to make a relationship work.

It won't be easy. It won't be quick. It won't be without pain. It won't be without patience. It won't be without frustration. It won't be without mistakes. It won't be without forgiveness. It won't be without apologizing. It won't be without tears.

But if you've found someone you love, it will be worth it if you can stick it out through all those challenges. Healing will come; redemption will come; trust, again, will come. Your heart can do it. It was made for love.

WE COME TO LOVE the things we do through a process. I wasn't born with an innate love of *Star Wars* (my friends might disagree)—I came to love it for a variety of reasons unique to my story as a person.

The scary thing is, I think we usually just accept what we love instead of asking ourselves "Should I love this thing?" or "Do I love this thing for healthy reasons?"

I recently had some time to kill and decided to fill out some lists on social media of books I've read, movies I've seen, and TV shows I've watched. I was feeling pretty good about myself when I was able to list over a hundred books I've read, but then came the over 300 movies and 150 TV shows I've watched. Wonder where a lot of my influence is coming from, huh?

We hate to admit we choose the things we love. We act instead as if our loves are the very definition of predestination, handed down by divine fiat from Valhalla. It speaks volumes that numerous Christians believe in some variation of the idea of a soul mate, someone who was made for each of us, even though this idea comes from Greek mythology and has no Christian basis.

That's not to say we aren't attracted to particular things or people more so than we are others, because of course we are. But to love something or someone—that's a choice. Despite strong feelings we may have, we decide how we act, which means we decide what we love.

This is really important to understand because it runs counter to the narrative we hear from culture. And it means we don't have to embrace some form of fatalistic idea of our life by believing "I love what I love, and there's nothing I can do about it."

This is the whole point behind the idea of discipleship, that we are formed through various disciplines into an intentional kind of person. Christian discipleship is meant to form people who are a lot like Jesus.

So, we really ought to take some time to examine what, exactly, the things we love are, because those things are influencing how we understand our identity.

WHAT DO WE MEAN by identity? What do we mean when we ask, "Who am I?"

Most of us are referring to our personalities—what we love, what we like, whether we're introverted or extroverted. And we become passionate about these personality traits because our culture tells us they are vital to who we are.

I disagree. I don't think these traits are intrinsic. So much of our personalities and preferences are learned behaviors that can be unlearned. They're important, but when I talk of identity, I want something concrete—beyond "Who am I?" and moving toward "What am I?"

Our culture is humanistic in orientation, which means we focus on human-centric, materialistic beliefs that elevate our own importance. We default to humanism in a lot of our thoughts without realizing it because we've been saturated with it our entire lives. Humanism assumes a kind of atheism, and there's an inescapable logical result when you boil it down to its philosophical foundations.

If there is no god(s) and humanism is right, then the only thing preventing us from doing whatever we want whenever we want are societies, and if you don't give a fig what other people think about you or what the repercussions are to what you do, then there is nothing to stop you from flaunting society's rules.

It's a deep rabbit hole, but if there is no god(s), then morality is just a social agreement we've all decided to follow. There is nothing inherently wrong or good about anything. We've just all come to a collective consensus that some things are good and other things are bad.

And in our individualistic age, who can say society has anything right? Most of us seem to rely on majority public opinion on any given topic even though we see people get things wrong all the time. So why do we place any faith in public opinion being correct? From this point of view, Nietzsche was right—triumph belongs to those who have the will to seize it, to bend the world toward their desires.

That's the basic philosophy that led to the rise of Nazism and underlies much of our contemporary culture. Freed from the chains of social convention, Nietzsche encouraged people to realize life is what we make it.

This is why so many people suffer identity crises—we don't know who the heck we are because we've been conditioned to think humanity is just another animal who happened upon the universe, so our identity is whatever we want to make it.

Like it or not, we all worship something because we all look for something to give our life meaning—our identity. And when culture tells us our life is about "me" because there is no greater meaning other than whatever it is "I" want, then suddenly my opinions and preferences become much more than just opinions and preferences—suddenly I'm heavily invested in them because these are mine, and that's all I have. This must be who I am, this must by my identity, how dare anyone question it?

There is, however, an alternative. Perhaps our identity as humans is found by realizing we are here for a purpose, that there is more to the universe than meets the eye. If we believe we have a purpose, suddenly all sorts of things stop having a death-grip on our self conceptions.

Suddenly I don't—primarily—identify myself by my race, my gender, my sexuality, my opinions, my preferences, my personality, because I realize—while these things are important—they aren't who I truly am. They aren't my primary identity, because that is only wrapped up in who God made me to be, and maybe—since we are all human—in some important way, we all have the same basic identity.

WHEN YOU GET DOWN to it, it's disagreements about how we determine our identity that are driving a lot of the discord in Western culture. It often feels like many of us are living in different realities from one another, perceiving events so distinctly that it's as if we're on separate worlds. Just what is going on?

I suspect we are living in the middle of the largest Western cultural revolution since the Protestant Reformation over 500 years ago. Whereas that era wrestled over the nature of the church and how we ought to interact with it and God, the present era is struggling with what it means to be human.

For hundreds of years, Western culture has slowly relocated power away from groups, institutions, and tradition toward individuals. A movement that began with the birth of the Renaissance and runs through the Reformation to the Enlightenment to the modern and postmodern eras has elevated the sovereignty of every individual. It's a natural and logical progression that has resulted in a culture that empowers the individual to define for his or herself who they are as humans in every respect.

That's one side of Western culture. But the other side represents the more ancient way of being human, of looking to the authority of others and holding a higher opinion of religious and cultural tradition.

Whichever side you and I fall on, I suggest, will be determined by how we view authority in deciding what is true and real.

The question of whether God is real is fundamental to understanding what it means to be human. It stands to reason that if there is a God who created us, that God may have done so with a purpose in mind. If that is true, then contrary to individualism, you and I aren't in charge of determining who we are: God is.

That's a really big deal, because the kind of individualism Western culture has come to believe in assumes one of two things: either God empowers individuals to determine who we are for ourselves (or, alternatively, God doesn't care about anything we do), or God doesn't exist. Because if God is real and has purposes for each of us, then we have no grounds for acting as gods in defining who we are. So, really, what we believe about God ought to likewise determine what we believe about ourselves.

The tension therefore exists between one stream of Western culture that is following individualism to its natural ends and one that isn't. Very broadly speaking, these streams are identified as "liberal" and "conservative" (and I'm not talking about in an American political sense).

In sum, those who typically align with conservatives are concerned that liberals are playing god with some really important and defining questions of human identity, while those who typically align with liberals are concerned that conservatives are only interested in denying people what they perceive to be their rights to choose who and what they want to be.

From this foundation flows many different streams that are full of nuance and a billion complicating factors, making our situation far more confusing and intricate than a simple dichotomy.

Let's reframe this not as an academic analysis but in the mode championed in this book: as stories. What is ultimately going on is the competition between two kinds of stories that are telling us in very different ways what it means to be human.

One story claims to be the tale that's been told by Judeo-Christianity for thousands of years regarding what it means to be human: God created us with a purpose in mind, and it's by trying to be what we were made to be that we understand what our identity is.

The other story implicitly accepts that either there is no God that created us or, if there is, we were created not to look to God for purpose but instead to make our purpose ourselves: that we are in essence in complete control and have freedom and power to understand who we are in whatever ways we want.

I think the solution to our cultural crisis is simply one of clarity in communication: of clearly understanding that our divisions are a result of this competition between two metanarratives regarding our human identity.

If we recognize that this is at the heart of the conflict, I think it will help us empathize better with one another and better grasp why the stakes feel so high. Because when you feel like your entire way of living is under attack or threat, you are going to respond aggressively, which is what we see happening all around us.

One of the principal problems is both sides in this conflict often seek to delegitimize and destroy the other rather than learning to accept each other and coexist.

But if we clearly articulate where we are coming from, peaceful coexistence is possible. There is a way for the non-discriminatory versions of both the liberal and conservative views of humanity to have space to exist, where both views aren't seeking to destroy the other but instead accept one another and work to live together.

While at the end of the day both viewpoints can't both be true, both do reflect logical progressions and make sense: if God is real and has a purpose for us, it makes sense as conservatives believe that trying to act out God's purpose is what it really means to be human; on the other hand, if either there is no God or if God has empowered us to have final say on our identity, it makes sense that the traditional ways we've had of understanding ourselves don't truly have any real hold on us other than what we choose to give them.

In this way, we can see that what we are currently experiencing is just another variation of a clash between different religious views that humanity has been experiencing throughout history. The difference is, this time, we ought to be equipped to recognize the reality of our situation while there is still time to act, and we ought to be able to extend love, grace, and space to those with whom we disagree.

6

THE STRUGGLE

When life gets me down, I sometimes feel frustrated with God. That frustration often revolves around our relationship.

In relating to God, if you believe Christian theology, you have to start from the premise "I'm not God," which means much of the self-centered mindset we pick up from living in Western culture has to be tossed out the window. We have to admit we aren't the most important person in the relationship.

Ergo, as "not God," the terms of our relationship aren't set by me, which kind of stinks because I like being in control.

I'm also frustrated by the thousands of Christian saints through the centuries who have had harder lives than I have yet have a much more intimate relationship with God. Why? How?

I think a lot of it comes down to choice. Making the right kinds of choices over and over eventually enables an ability to trust God and his goodness, sometimes despite our feelings. It bears repeating that one of the first choices we have to make, often several times a day, is to acknowledge "I am not God."

Our obsession over the individual and rights has resulted in our mass perception that "I" am the complete master of my life in all ways, shapes, and forms. Now don't get me wrong, our autonomy and rights are important. We just take them to extremes.

In truth, nothing is mine except for choice—our will—and even my choices are influenced by outside factors. We are finite, so whatever we call ours is in truth on loan to us for whatever amount of time we have in life: our possessions, our thoughts, our time aren't owned by us when we're dead (copyright laws notwithstanding).

In choosing to accept that I am not God, it follows that God doesn't owe me anything. What I mean by that is he isn't indebted to me. I struggle with this because it certainly feels to me like God owes me in this sense. This belief permeates a lot of society. We often feel like our parents owe us, our institutions owe us, our government owes us.

In some ways that's true, because holding each other accountable in a society to ensure basic needs and rights are met is morally right, so there are some things, in a manner of speaking, we are owed. But is using that kind of language the best way to describe the dynamic?

I think not, and the distinction has large ramifications. This is semantic, but the way we say something affects our perception. To say a parent owes anything to his or her child by default is incorrect: when my daughter was born, I was not put in debt to her. Should she expect me to provide certain things for her as a loving parent, things that would be criminally or morally negligent if I didn't provide them for her? Yes, of course. But it's incorrect to say I owe her.

To phrase things as being owed implicitly places the one claiming a debt in position of power. If I tell you that you owe me something, it has the effect of implementing a power dynamic. It implies there is a debt to be paid, a debt you incurred at my expense. To claim that by nature a parent owes anything to a child or God owes anything to us incorrectly alters the relational dynamic, placing the child in position of power over the parent and the creature in position of power over the Creator.

Much of my anger at God from my teens and twenties stems from this faulty way of understanding our relational dynamic. Without realizing it, I treated my relationship with God as a series of legal transactions: I do something for him and expect him to do what I want in return.

I understood my emotions and life experience in the same way. The amount of pain I experienced as a child during years of panic attacks, hopelessness, and despair created an intense feeling that God owed me at least as much joy, peace, and happiness. When I was met with more disappointment and pain instead of the joy I felt was my right, deep anger and resentment followed.

That said, I don't think it's true that one never has reason to be angry at God. The Psalms depict several angered outbursts at God, and Lamentations is a depressed, deep expression of grief. There's a place for expressing these emotions because, when you break everything down to its foundations, the universe is the way it is because God allows it to be, and sometimes that can lead to events that draw out all kinds of emotional responses.

The root causes of evil are the presence of a real enemy of God's (the "adversary," or the satan) and the ability granted by God to allow many of his creatures choice. Yet be that as it may, God still allows the universe to continue as it is.

But the difference between shaking our fist at the heavens and choosing to love and submit to God regardless is trust.

We have the option to trust God in light of what is revealed in Scripture and illuminated by the church. That revelation consists of this: God is not immune from the pain and suffering he allows, and God is in the process of ultimately taking all of it on himself. In the incarnation, God experiences what it is to be human as the man Jesus of Nazareth, and in the mystical reality of what occurred at the crucifixion, God takes upon himself the brunt of creation's brokenness.

I'm going to be brutally honest, though. Even if that's true, that means jack squat to me while in the midst of intense suffering. That's fantastic God, you're a masochist, so I have to suffer, too?

No. That is not the end of the promise. The end of the promise is that there is a purpose to this universe which will result in a reality so wonderful it will make our pain pale in comparison.

For me, that's a tough sale. My experience screams otherwise, because my intimacy with suffering often feels more intense than my familiarity with joy. But again, this comes down to a matter of trust: am I going to trust my own experience as one of billions upon billions of other humans with different experiences, or am I going to trust what God says?

Frankly, when push has come to shove, a lot of the time I've chosen to trust my experience. I've run from God because I have chosen to remain angry with him.

The psalmists and Jeremiah in Lamentations did not. They railed at God but always come out on the other side, choosing to trust in his undying love and goodness. The prime example of suffering, Job, chooses the same. Job is incredibly upset with God, yet never chooses to blaspheme him for what God has allowed to happen.

But it's interesting how God ultimately answers Job's pleas. For a long time, God's response made no sense to me because, as the words on the page read, God doesn't give an actual answer to Job's question of "Why?" God shows up and asks Job pages worth of variations on the theme of: "Are you me? Are you God? Do you know everything? Have you been around since before time?" And Job accepts this response! In essence he replies, "Yep, you're right, I'm not you, and I was wrong to think I could question you" (Job 38—42, my paraphrase).

Come again? For years I puzzled over this, telling myself that if that happened to me, I would never respond like Job. "No, God, I'm blasted well not you, but that doesn't mean I shouldn't get answers to my questions, does it?" Why does this satisfy Job? What about these words provides solace?

It isn't the words. It's the Word, God himself. God's presence. It's the fact God showed up. God himself is the answer. And God himself is the answer to all our questions, all our hurt, all our disillusionment.

We are made whole within relationship with God, which is a relationship with his corporate body the church and with his corporate body the Trinity.

Yet even knowing this, I still continue to struggle, because finding that intimacy with God right now in this life seems so flipping hard.

It's hard because God doesn't always show up in the ways we want him to. I've had really awesome spiritual highs, but I've also gone through periods of dryness, and a lot of the time neither the highs nor the lows had anything to do with me.

The Christian life isn't about grabbing all the goodies God wants to bless us with. God surely does want to bless us, but the ultimate blessing is himself. Not even the experience of himself; just straight up himself, even if I feel or receive nothing tangible.

That's a tough pill to swallow. It's hard because we have to persevere when God seems silent or distant, yet at the same time it's easy, because as long as we choose to keep seeking God, all the rest of the burden is on him to show up, to help us, to do his work for his church through us as we hold his hand.

There are practices that help cultivate an intimacy with God like regularly allowing him to speak through the reading of Scripture and seeking his voice in prayer. But there is no formula for forcing God's response. As C.S. Lewis wrote regarding Aslan in *The Lion, the Witch and the Wardrobe*, "He's not a tame lion."

That being the case, I sometimes get bored by the pursuit of God. Because God doesn't always show up in the ways I'd like him to, it's tempting to choose to stay home and play a video game rather than go to church. If we're fortunate enough to experience the highs of God's movement in our lives, it nevertheless easily fades into memory as time passes.

Eventually, though, we reach a point where there is a clear choice between directions in life. Do we continue to pursue the things that prove themselves to be empty but temporarily satisfying, or do we chase after that which can sometimes be temporarily unsatisfying but is ultimately fulfilling?

I have prematurely abandoned the pursuit of God in order to go after things that are immediately exciting but ultimately pointless. When I choose to reverse course and push through the initial boredom with God, I eventually see glimpses of deep joy and an undying land lying within reach.

But there is no final point of arrival for us while we're still breathing because temptations will always exist. The major internal shift comes when we realize how pointless most of the things we fill our life with are compared to choosing to pursue God. And as we realize that more deeply, and as we grow in our experience of feeling God's presence, the pursuit of God becomes more of a joyful thing.

As Brennan Manning puts it in the title of his book *Ruthless Trust*, it's indeed a ruthless trust we need to develop in God. God is faithful and trustworthy—this is gonna be worth it. Just hold on. The thing God wants the most is intimacy with us. That's what we have to pursue to begin experiencing and understanding real life.

I often return to the scene in the gospels between Jesus and the disciples after Jesus delivered a difficult teaching that caused most of those who were following him to turn away and leave. Jesus turns to his twelve closest friends and asks them, "You do not want to leave too, do you?" To which Peter gives the seminal response, "Lord, to whom shall we go? You have the words of eternal life" (John 6:67–68).

What vulnerability Jesus shows. "Are you going to leave me, too?" I often imagine him asking me the same question whenever I get frustrated. I turn and look at the other options I could choose and, after weighing their merits, turn to face him and reply, "Where else am I going to go? You're the only one I was made for."

God is in the business of drawing us to him. That's what this life's about, responding to God's call to enter into intimacy with him. The peaks and valleys are all about growing closer to him through thick and thin, for richer and for poorer, in sickness and in health, so that nothing will cause us to part from one another.

It's learning to trust. A ruthless and radical trust, the kind of trust that can withstand anything. Not a blind trust without reason, but the trust that is developed between two people over decades of facing everything life can throw at us. God is there, holding out his hand, not asking you to summon trust out of thin air, but asking you to begin the journey toward learning that kind of trust.

I'VE WRESTLED WITH ONE of the central questions posed to God in the Psalms and Job—why, God, if you're real and you're good, is there evil?

We don't know. God knows of course, but instead of explaining in words, he answers in action. That's not always satisfying to me. I don't want God right next to me, hurting with me; I want the hurting to stop. But it often doesn't.

I've been angry at God because, if he is all knowing and all powerful and created all things, then he is culpable for evil and suffering. But I've realized that's only true if evil is actually a thing in itself. Just as darkness may simply be nothing but the absence of light, perhaps evil is simply the absence of good.

If that is close to the truth, God didn't make evil, per se. If God is goodness, then whatever is anti-God is also anti-good.

Nonetheless, God is still responsible for allowing anti-good things to exist. This is fortunate in a way because there is both anti-goodness and goodness at the core of every human heart, so we might not be here if God didn't tolerate it. But then we can ask God the legitimate question, "Why did you make me this way?"

We don't have an answer. Maybe it has to do with love requiring choice, and there has to be an option to reject love if true love is going to be possible. But then we can wonder why love has to be that way. God made love, so why not make it different?

Maybe, though, love, like evil, isn't a thing itself. Maybe it's just a natural part of who God is. If God is triune, existing in eternal self-sufficient love within the relationship of the Trinity, then love is just the natural result of God existing. And maybe if God wants to reproduce that kind of love in life outside the Trinity, this is how it has to start out.

That's a thought that helps some. But if I didn't believe deep down God's plan is somehow going to work in the end, it wouldn't help at all. But I do choose to believe that, though I'm not sure I can explain why—how I can be both angry at why things are the way they are but still trust when it's all said and done it's going to work. But I do—it's just the process in the meantime I sometimes hate.

And I think God hates it, too. I think he's right there with me, saying in essence: "Yes. Parts of life right now are terrible. No, it's not OK. It will work in the end, though. All will be made right, and you'll see. I know it's hard. Trust me."

And the cross helps me here. It shows that evil is personal to God; it's not some problem like inflation or a rainy day—it's the gaping wound in God's side, a knife constantly twisting. Because on the cross God let evil bring its worst on him, and on the cross he defeated it. Though the battle rages on, the war has been won. And the cross has been passed to me as part of Christ's church.

The message of the cross as it applies to me is, with Christ in me, I stand in the gaps where evil still carries on its battles just as Christ stood in the gap to win the ultimate war. I don't stand on my own power but with Christ in me and the church by my side. I'm not in this alone.

The embrace of the cross is more than accepting salvation. It's taking up Jesus' way of life. It's expecting to suffer. It's expecting to confront evil. It's knowing that this is my vocation as a disciple, to be Christ in the world. And it's coming to terms with the fact that it's quite probable that in my confrontations with evil, by all outward appearances it will look and feel like evil wins.

For three days it seemed like the forces of darkness had fought God, and God lost. That the darkness actually was, in fact, stronger. Three days. An eternity if you're living it. But through the very process in which evil sought to conquer and destroy, it was defeated. Certain victory was blindsided by crushing defeat.

And that is our path, as well. Not masochistic. Just not shocked when evil and pain seem to find us. And not overcome with despair, but being able to rejoice as the apostles did because the arrival of evil is proof we are succeeding in our vocation—evil is being drawn to us, and through Christ in us it is being destroyed even when it may look like utter catastrophe.

I think that was Paul's and the apostles' secret: they really did learn to see their life that way. That's how they could sing in prison. How they could count their persecution as joy. It seems so utterly alien, but it's so very true.

I'M BEGINNING TO WONDER if a way of viewing faith I have long been at odds with may have some truth to it. Being an over-analytical book worm, I have recoiled at Christians who talk of faith as if it's blind. I've countered with Peter's exhortation to be prepared to give the reasons for why we have the hope that we do (1 Pet 3:15).

I grew up on apologetics. I was intellectually compelled to make the Christian faith of my parents my own because I became convinced it was most likely the true depiction of reality. Faith, I've always thought, isn't blind.

I've been revisiting the work of nineteenth-century philosopher Soren Kierkegaard, one of the first existentialists and also a devout Christian. One of his famous statements about Christianity is it requires a person to make a leap of faith. I was flabbergasted when I first read this and couldn't understand how such a brilliant thinker could write something so dumb.

Now I think I'm starting to pick up what he was putting down. What if the leap of faith a person must make to be a Christian isn't about believing whether God exists? What if it's about believing he is good?

The Good Christian Answer is we have God's promises in Scripture to fall back on as evidence of his goodness. But as the saying goes, "What have you done for me lately?" Not to be flippant, but all that stuff is well and good, and I believe it, but it hasn't happened in my life. I believe it happened for me, but I haven't seen it.

But blast it, Jesus told Thomas those who don't see and believe are blessed (John 20:29), so what am I supposed to do?

While I do have the promises of Scripture, and I can maybe one day see the miraculous hand of God still at work that many Christians claim to witness, in the face of disappointment and life dreams that are either delayed or will go unfulfilled, I must stand and insist God is good. It *is* going to work out. The price I pay—we all pay—*will* be worth it. Everything this life has to offer *does* pale in comparison for what is yet to come.

Because I have reason to believe the promises of Scripture. And Jesus told me there that if those like me don't believe the prophets that came before, we aren't going to believe any miraculous signs, either.

Now I just have to keep reminding myself of this and praying for God to give me the grace to feel it deep within my bones.

HOW WILL GOD ACTUALLY go about making everything right with the world through Christ?

I suggested earlier evil may be best understood as the absence of good, the absence of God. Building more on that thought, evil would be personal to God. It would be like a wound. Because in the Trinity there is perfect love, acceptance, and commitment, anything other than this wounds God. If we view evil in this way, it looks the way it does because this is what it looks like when God is hurt.

That is why rejection of God (rebellion; sin) has negative consequences—it alters the foundations of existence, because the only foundation on which everything else is built is God himself. Because God is the basis of our existence, to reject God is to reject also who we ourselves truly are.

We were created to be in relationship with God, in union with him as he within the Trinity is in union with himself. This is why we exist, whether we like it or not or choose to accept it or not. We have no ability to change the essence of who we are.

For evil to end—for God's wound to heal and reality to return to its intended state—rejection of God (sin) must end. Instead of choosing to eliminate the creatures causing sin, God chooses to become his wound himself—to embody his own rejection—so that those who injured him could continue to exist with him in perfected reality.

And God does this because he loves us. Not because he was lonely—he was fulfilled within the Trinity—but because the natural result of love is a movement outward to expand love. True love is so good that by nature those experiencing it are compelled to increase it. Where we experience pure joy, we want others to share it, just as humans in love create new life to expand the love of a family.

Love is part of who God is, and part of love's nature is unity. In pure love one person completely shares the life of another. This is how the Trinity lives love. The Father is in the Son as the Son is in the Father and as both are in the Holy Spirit. What one person experiences, the others do, too.

Once evil became a part of reality, those united in love united in experiencing evil. And there's the rub. While God's wound continues to heal, all of creation is subject to the same ramifications God is subject to, though God took the brunt of it on the cross.

All of humanity, even those who reject God, remain at least latently connected to him due to the nature of who we are: creatures created to exist in relation with God. Unless God severs that connection completely, we all by our nature—and the rest of creation as subject to humanity—share in God's experience. We get glimpses of the joy that is his joy and the pain that is his pain.

For those who intentionally choose to unite with God in love, our share in his full experience can be intensified: our joys more joyful yet our sorrows more painful because we more directly connect to reality.

Could this be the answer to why we suffer? Because if we are to love, we have to experience all that our lover does? And our lover continues to suffer in order that we may join in his ultimate joy?

Could this be why Christians are told to pick up our cross and follow Jesus? Why we are to count it joy to share in his sufferings?

Because we know we are drawing closer to him in love by sharing in what he feels?

Instead of being angry at God when we hurt, should we be filled with compassion? Because we know our pain is only a small fraction of what God continues to endure for our sake?

Should our perception of evil and suffering not be indignation that God allows it to exist but, in some bizarre way, thankfulness mixed with mourning because—while it in itself is terrible—it is not yet fully eliminated in order to allow love to continue to expand?

Is evil's continued existence a terrible and lamentable yet necessary example of God's mercy and compassion toward us? And while it is right to mourn and fight it, should we not in proper time be thankful for the experience of sharing this with God because it means our love is genuine and our unity with God is increasing?

Christ, our pain is your pain, your pain is our pain. Because we love you and want to share life with you. Bring all people to you, Father, quickly, so that evil may finally end and our joy be made complete. And may we submit ourselves to be extensions of you, with you in us, toward this end. In Christ's name, may it be so.

FALLING ACTION

O ver a year of consistent cleaning has passed, and the efforts have revealed that my great-grandfather's tombstone is pure white in color. All the stains are gone, and some small carvings emerged around the inscription of his name.

The results are better than I could have hoped for. Now I just have to try to fit the broken pieces together again.

All the wisdom Google can find tells me the best way to repair an old tombstone is to use special epoxy and mortar instead of trying to insert internal supports that would damage the integrity of the stone.

After layering the crevices of both broken pieces with epoxy, I set them together and apply two braces to hold them firmly in place while everything dries.

The epoxy isn't intended to withstand rain and snow, so after it dries for a week, I use a rotary tool to hollow out ridges along the edges of the seal to cover it in preservation mortar that can withstand the elements.

After all that sets, it's back to Ohio to return it to its home and pray the repairs last.

ONE OF THE MANY things they don't prepare you for as a kid is the applause and affirmation to stop. You don't win many awards, get recognition, compliments, or words of encouragement when you're an adult. And if you've started to rely on those things as a child, their absence is like a punch in the gut.

By my mid-twenties, I was bluntly faced with harsh realities. Since my pre-teen years, I'd understood myself to be a devoted Christian with a fair amount of talent who was going to live life the right way and do huge things for the Kingdom of God. At age twenty-six, my faith was on life-support, I had wasted my talents, thought I'd ruined my life and the life of my child by failing to keep a relationship with her mother, and accomplished absolutely nothing in life.

I felt like the silent jury of my peers and the world at large which had provided the affirmation I'd grown to rely on saw me as a straight up loser. A waste. Owner of a useless degree with no prospects, no love, no money, and no hope. Every lie I'd learned by rote as a child in panic gathered strength as voices in my head: "Look at yourself, you're pathetic. You can't do anything right. All the talent in the world and you do absolutely nothing. What will people say and think about you?"

God, if he was there, dangled one last life line, the friend I'd made at my now-lost job and the group of guys I'd befriended who seemed to have a lot in common with me. So, broken, I started going to their church to give God one more chance.

It was very different from my experience as an evangelical Methodist—high church Anglican, with a lot of the trappings of Catholicism. Alien, but intriguing in its difference.

I'd found some semblance of life years before while exploring church history and learning about ancient Christian practice. I'd thought if anyone had life to them, it would've been the people closest to the time of the disciples, so maybe this old stuff had some legitimacy to it.

This particular church was peculiar though, not for its high liturgical worship, but because its priest preached like a Baptist, and it believed the Holy Spirit still did the things Scripture claimed he did back in the day, namely, healing and empowering people. This was what I'd imagined an alive church would look like, to be seeking the power of God as described in Scripture.

So, you're up God, what do you have? God had a lot of prayer by a lot of different people. Prayer for the Holy Spirit to heal my heart, my mind, my soul, my history. Prayer during Sunday worship; prayer by special appointments; and identifying beliefs I had about myself that, according to Scripture, were lies.

I learned there is head knowledge and there is heart knowledge. All I'd known was head knowledge, the stuff you learn by reading books and hearing people lecture and remembering facts. I knew a lot of things in my head about God and thought that was all there was to it. But it's not.

Trust involves the mind and the heart. And the wounds of a seven-year-old boy who felt left out in the cold by God were in my heart.

You remember that scene in *Good Will Hunting*, the one near the end when Robin Williams repeats over and over to Matt Damon "It's not your fault," and at first Damon's like, "Yeah, of course, I know it's not my fault," but Robin Williams keeps saying it again and again until Damon breaks down sobbing? I like that movie, but I used to think that was the stupidest part until I realized that's a decent way of depicting the moment when head knowledge finally makes its way to the heart.

I'd heard my whole life that Jesus loves me, God loves me, God forgives me, God is always with me. I knew it in my head like I know the difference between night and day. But I didn't know it in my heart. I didn't believe it in my heart.

And, funny thing about your thoughts, and you may not believe me on this part, but that's OK. If the thoughts you have in your head are anything like mine, you hear them in your own voice. I have a running dialogue with myself as I go about my day. And a lot of it is unintentional and just habit—like I stub my toe and some random thought like, "Great job, idiot" will just pop in there.

But start paying attention to your thoughts. Pay really close attention. Everything is in your voice, but, in my case, you start to sense that some of the thoughts have a different character to them than others. That's undeniably true in many cases—we typically internalize a lot of the things our parents or guardians spoke over us as part of our own running dialogue.

But if the Christian metanarrative is indeed true, and there is a spiritual war going on around us that we're largely blind to, wouldn't it make sense that some of the thoughts in our heads come from somewhere else, and possibly somewhere else that means us harm?

I've noticed it with myself. I started to pick out the differences between thoughts that came from my mom or dad, thoughts that I know come from me, thoughts I know are memories from things I recall from Scripture, and thoughts that are characteristically distinct and dark, that I'd assumed were me. The thoughts I quoted above: "Look at yourself, you're pathetic. You can't do anything right. All the talent in the world and you do absolutely nothing. What will people say and think about you?" Huh.

All of this was, really, a form of cognitive reconditioning, where we retrain our mind what to think and focus on. And it uses Scripture as its foundation, which is also used to correct errors in the metanarrative we've crafted to live our lives by. The grounding for truth is in Scripture and what the church has taught about who we are as people for 2,000 years—everything else that argues against those truths is either a distortion or a lie.

Over many sessions and much prayer, I called out the lies I'd internalized and voiced the truth in their place, and in the process, I learned better the character of Jesus and what he would say to me. Now, mind you, as I started doing this, part of me felt like an idiot and thought the whole thing was ridiculous. But that's Intellectual David who's too smart for something that looks so dumb—when I shut him up, it worked.

I learned to recognize the lies and stop them in their tracks in my head. Even when part of me believed a lie, I chose to believe more firmly in Scripture. And I eventually got into the weeds, the real hardcore junk, as I learned to know what God says to that garbage.

So it was that, slowly, the template of my mind changed to reject the lies I'd picked up over the years and replace them with the truths of God's love for me. And it's not done, not by a long shot, nor will it ever be fully done, for we continually face hardships in life.

Slowly my heart, and not just my head, began to believe God loves me, that I'm special to him. I still call it into question a lot more than I'd like to admit, and there is still the nagging thought that likes to creep in the back of my head that it's all a lie and sham, but I've seen enough in life to know we are indeed at war, and I recognize the voice whispering those thoughts.

Jesus said in the Gospel of John that he came to give us life, and to give it abundantly (John 10:10), and that life, just like the Kingdom of God, is here, now. Not "in heaven." Here. Now. As demonstrated over and over in the gospels, Jesus wants to heal the wounded, physically and emotionally.

And the thing is, the condemnation I gave myself from my imaginary jury of peers and the world, that I haven't done what I set out to do, that I haven't changed the world or made a lot of money or made a name for myself . . . well, that's true. I sure haven't. I've made mistakes. I still do. I have indeed squandered my talents, not fulfilled my potential to its utmost. I fail, and I fail quite a bit.

But haven't we all, whether the world sees those things or they remain hidden from public sight? And, there isn't condemnation for any of that. Zero. "Therefore, there is now no condemnation for those who are in Christ Jesus" (Rom 8:1). I fight to believe it, but there's only one jury whose approval matters, and it consists of one all-loving God.

And as I trudge through life clinging to God and refusing to let go no matter how many times I fall down and get back up, that's all that matters. I don't know why, because I don't understand the true depths of grace, but he's in love with me as I am, day in and day out. He accepts me. All I can do is rest in him, fill my heart and head with the only affirmations that truly fulfill, learn to take my strength from the indwelling of the Holy Spirit, and take one day at a time.

1

FROM A CERTAIN POINT OF VIEW

We discussed a bit before about our beliefs being motivated by what we love and what we want, and I want to dig a little deeper into that. I suspect all of us can think of times when we realized we'd chosen to believe something even while we knew we weren't being honest with ourselves.

I was skeptical when I first heard someone suggest that our beliefs are connected to our wants, desires, and loves. But the more I considered it, the more it made sense. It also spoke to my nerd heart by helping me better understand a pivotal plot shift in my favorite movie series.

I'm banking on you having at least a vague knowledge of the major themes of the six *Star Wars* movies before Disney's recent, concluding trilogy. In short—the original three made in the 1970s and 1980s were primarily the story of the redemption of a character who appeared to be completely evil, Darth Vader. The next three movies were prequels which chronologically began forty years before the first three to show how a good person, Anakin Skywalker, can become evil, showing how he became Vader.

I prefer the original trilogy to the prequels, but I still appreciate them, especially the concluding prequel, *Revenge of the Sith.* For a long time, I was dissatisfied with the way this movie seemed to depict Anakin's turn to evil like it was the flip of a switch. Now, I think it depicts a key human tendency.

Star Wars is a morality tale that asks questions about the nature of good and evil, where the lines are drawn between each, and how we are compelled to be the kinds of people we become. It takes place in a fictional galaxy with different physical laws. There is a mystical connection between all life called the Force, and certain people are born with an ability to tap into the powers of the Force and perform spectacular physical and mental feats.

A religious/warrior caste devoted to doing good through use of the Force is called the Jedi. A similar caste devoted to pursuing power and imposing order is called the Sith. Light and dark; good and bad.

Anakin is seemingly a child born of Jedi prophecy, conceived in his mother by the Force in order to bring a balance between the light and dark. He is discovered by the Jedi in the first prequel as a ten-year-old boy living as a slave. He has a powerful connection with the Force, but his life as a slave has fostered a great deal of fear inside him, which initially make the Jedi hesitant to train him as one of their own.

Anakin is depicted as a kind-hearted boy whom grows into a powerful Jedi, caring a great deal about justice and order. The other prequels show how Anakin's deep passion and love for his friends and family are centered around a core of selfishness: he is afraid to lose those he loves and shows a great deal of possessiveness because he doesn't want to experience the pain associated with loss.

The temptation for Anakin is that he is powerful enough with the Force that he might be able to control life and death itself, but trying to do so is opposed to Jedi teachings. The stage for Anakin's fall is set when doubts are raised in his mind about who the Jedi really are. He begins to question their motives, and this questioning is driven in large part by his growing desire to become more powerful in order to prevent a vision of a tragedy from coming true.

What had troubled me about Anakin's decision to leave the Jedi and join the Sith was how quickly it seemed to happen. But when we view our knowledge, beliefs, and motivations as rising from our loves and desires more than from our intellectual processes, this makes sense: the core of who Anakin was—what he wanted, what he loved—had always been tainted.

His deepest desires were selfish. In his heart, he wanted to control all aspects of his life because he loved out of attachment and personal need, not out of a place that considered the intrinsic worth of others. These core desires fought against the ideals of the community he associated with, and by allowing his desires to trump his morals, his beliefs changed.

I think this is a realistic portrait of internal struggles within all of us that at any moment can also abruptly surface and give the appearance that a very sudden change has occurred. How many times have we heard friends and loved ones of people who commit terrible crimes say, "That's not the person I knew. He [or she] was always so nice and pleasant to talk to" or something similar? In reality a struggle was being waged internally, sometimes subconsciously, and maybe for just one horrific moment, the wrong desire won out.

Anakin's choice to fuel his controlling desires directly impacted his outlook, beliefs, and knowledge. He interpreted events at the end of *Revenge of the Sith* as attempts by the Jedi to gain more power for themselves. Suddenly he "knew" that he had been lied to during his entire training, and in "reality" the Jedi—not the Sith—were trying to cause turmoil and disorder.

Instead of seeing his training as an attempt at teaching him how to find life by giving his own in service of something greater than himself, he now perceived that the Jedi were trying to rob him of what was rightfully his—his raw power and personal will—because they didn't want to lose their own power to him.

One of the important truths we need to understand is that there aren't good people and bad people in this world: there are only people who choose to be influenced by different desires. We all have the same ones floating around within us that are enticing us to take steps that lead down certain kinds of paths.

The paths we travel mold us in certain ways: some good, some bad. Some things that at first seem innocent begin journeys down dangerous paths and can result in us aligning ourselves with evil.

What wants and desires are you choosing to empower? How are those directing your knowledge, your beliefs, and your life?

I'VE SPILLED MY GUTS to you because sharing life is the best way any of us grow and learn. As hopefully becomes more obvious to us as we age and mature, people are complicated. Likely owing to the self-scrutiny that came from the panic episodes I experienced in childhood, one of my interests has been in researching just what, exactly, makes us tick.

I've dabbled as a layman in psychology, neuroscience, ethics, philosophy, theology, and world religions. What is it that makes me a Christian, that guy over there a Muslim, that lady over there an atheist?

It isn't easy to pinpoint, because it's not a single thing. It's not just ideas. It's life experience. It's also—and we hate to hear this—emotion.

As children of Western culture, the Enlightenment continues to have a huge impact on how we think, but the devastation of two world wars called our views of life and knowledge drastically into question. After so much death, destruction, and evil, how could we have any confidence we truly knew what we were doing? The philosophy known as postmodernism developed as a result.

As I've said, postmodernism did us the favor of identifying that each of us live our lives according to a story, a narrative. Basically, we're told by some form of an institution (be that your family, your church, your state, or something else) how to understand life, what you're supposed to believe about yourself and the world around you. This story that governs your life is a metanarrative—a controlling story.

Using myself as an example, my metanarrative is Christianity because, by Christian belief, I interpret myself and the world around me. This is oversimplified, but basically, when I make a moral mistake, I view it as sin because that's what the church has taught me to believe. When something good happens to me, I view it as a blessing because that's what the church has taught me to believe.

Postmodernists call all metanarratives into question and basically shout "Viva la revolución!" in response. Down with the metanarratives! They're all created by people and institutions who are trying to control us, to exert power over us. Recognize how we're trying to be duped and call shenanigans on it.

And in some instances, true enough! Nation-states throughout human history have definitely fed their people lines of garbage to get them to comply to their desires, and the church has unfortunately been as guilty of doing it as anyone.

But, peer closely at the rhetoric of postmodernists and you note a peculiarity—the claim that all metanarratives are out to get us is, itself, a metanarrative.

Let's maybe pull back a little bit on the pitchforks and torches, perhaps, and note that we as humans just by nature tend to understand our place in the world according to stories.

In a hyper-individualistic society like the post-industrial West, it's typically "I," and not an institution, who is writing that controlling narrative. We make up our own way more often than not. And I'd question the wisdom in that, because I sure as heck know I can be a dufus—I need the help and wisdom of other people.

But something feels right, doesn't it, to decide for yourself what you want to do? You feel empowered and can do what you want and choose to believe in the consequences (or not) that you think may follow.

Well, there's a problem with that. What if you're wrong? What if the cumulative thought of the last 500 years has led us to rely too much on our individualism, and we've lost our way?

Because, here's the truth: while we definitely use our brains, what we choose to believe as true about the world is not just an intellectual exercise. It's not even primarily one. It's a result of our wants, desires, and unhealed wounds—we're emotional creatures.

I quoted this before but to reiterate, "What the heart desires, the will chooses, and the mind justifies." To explain more in-depth the thought behind this statement, here's Dr. Ashley Null from a September 2001 interview with *Anglican Church League News*:

> What the heart loves, the will chooses, and the mind justifies. The mind doesn't direct the will. The mind is actually captive to what the will wants, and the will itself, in turn, is captive to what the heart wants. The trouble with human nature is that we are born with a heart that loves ourselves over and above everything else in this world, including God. In short, we are born slaves to the lust for self-gratification . . . That's why, if left to ourselves, we will always love those things that make us feel good about ourselves, even as we depart more and more from God and his ways. Therefore, God must intervene in our lives in order to bring salvation.

Obviously, that's a Christian quote and train of thought. But, remove "God" from that quote and it's still true, isn't it? We do lust after self-gratification. It's our natural religion.

So, just how in the world do we know what to believe about truth, about life? We can't trust our brain to go about picking out what's true because our heart and our will (impacted by our—likely damaged and traumatized—emotions) are probably going to throw us off.

Man, I wrestled with this for years. I'm not going to pretend like I have a perfect answer, because life is complicated and hard, and people disagree for a ton of reasons.

But Jesus saved me from myself, from my own brokenness. And there are reasons you could question whether it was actually Jesus who saved me or just good psychology. There's also no reason both answers can't be true.

A lot of the things that saved me are indeed a form of cognitive behavioral therapy, a way of retraining the brain how to think, and also a use of narrative therapy, a psychological practice that analyzes the metanarrative we've chosen to believe and replaces it with a healthier version. But there's also been prayer. There's also been spiritual experiences that defy easy, cookie-cutter explanations.

There is some truth to individualism, and one of those truths is this: it's up to you how you're going to choose to interpret reality, no matter what I or anyone else say or do. I can only share my heart and mind with you and, from my perspective, pray that God starts doing for you some of the things he's done (and, good God, still need doing) in me. And also try to express to you, whomever you are, that I truly believe you are worth loving. I really do.

I'VE SHARED MOST OF my life's story about how Christ healed me, and I've shared along the way why I believe Christianity is true. But so what? Being healed from trauma and my own brokenness sure beats continuing to go around bleeding all over everyone I love, but why does God place an emphasis on healing? What's he up to?

In a word: redemption. Redemption is one of three large themes I think God has been writing in his tale, and these themes serve as the meaning of life. If the Christian God is the author of everything in existence, then this is his play, and we are part of the cast.

What his ultimate purpose is remains a mystery, but we know at least three themes will be eternally important: redemption, war, and love, and love is the centerpiece. These three are interwoven, for it's God's love that motivates redemption, and redemption is necessary because we are at war.

The Fall of humanity as depicted in Genesis, whether historical or allegorical, is more than simply Adam and Eve betraying God by eating forbidden fruit—they are tricked into this act in the midst of a war by God's enemy as depicted as the serpent, the deceiver, the satan.

We don't know why there is a war. We don't know why an all-powerful God permits the continued existence of evil. We just know that there is a war, and the corruption of humanity came as a result of it.

As caretakers of creation, with humanity's Fall, the rest of creation also fell into death and decay. To understand the full spiritual significance of the cross is to understand Christ's central role in reversing the Fall, reversing Adam's mistake, and not only making a way for each of us to reestablish communion with God, but likewise all of creation.

> The creation waits in eager expectation for the sons of God to be revealed. For the creation was subjected to frustration, not by its own choice, but by the will of the one who subjected it, in hope that the creation itself will be liberated from its bondage to decay and brought into the glorious freedom of the children of God. We know that the whole creation has been groaning as in the pains of childbirth right up to the present time. Not only so, but we ourselves, who have the firstfruits of the Spirit, groan inwardly as we wait eagerly for our adoption as sons, the redemption of our bodies. For in this hope we are saved (Rom 8:19–24).

It's the Christian's job, therefore, to be agents of redemption, to work to facilitate the healing of ourselves and the earth. This earth was entrusted to our care, and we're to be instruments in bringing about its restoration. Redeeming our fellow man and our environment is not optional.

The Christian also cannot ignore that we continue to be at war. Scripture promises this war was won by Christ and is only yet awaiting the final stroke to fall, but until that time, battles rage on. To my detriment, I long believed I could be a bystander on the sidelines while the fighting went on around me, but there are no bystanders in a battle. Either you're prepared to fight, or you'll be plowed over in the heat of combat. But we are not fighting our fellow man.

> Finally, be strong in the Lord and in his mighty power. Put on the full armor of God so that you can take your stand against the devil's schemes. For our struggle is not against flesh and blood, but against the rulers, against the authorities, against the powers of this dark world and against the spiritual forces of evil in the heavenly realms (Eph 6:10–12).

Perhaps if I'd understood this truth more clearly and deeply as a child, my panic episodes would have taken on a different context—the enemy was not, as I believed, myself, a lie I allowed to bore deep within my soul and alter my self-understanding. I was being attacked. The thoughts and fear did not originate only with me.

Learn to see your own struggles in the same way. Surely we do bring a lot of trouble on ourselves, but much of what we are fighting against is not directly a result of self or other people, but rather the influences the powers of darkness are directing at both. The correct response to win our fights is to confront those powers head on.

But where the war will one day finally be over and redemption will be complete, love is forever. Love is not God, but God is love, and love properly understood encapsulates both redemption and war—we engage in these out of love and because of love. I am moved to work for redemption and to fight against darkness to free myself and others because of love. Love is an abundantly clear cornerstone of Scripture.

> 'Teacher, which is the greatest commandment in the Law?' Jesus replied: 'Love the Lord your God with all your heart and with all your soul and with all your mind. This is the first and greatest commandment. And the second is like it: Love your neighbor as yourself. All the Law and the Prophets hang on these two commands (Matt 22:36–40).

Let no debt remain outstanding, except the continuing debt to love one another, for he who loves his fellow-man has fulfilled the law. The commandments, 'Do not commit adultery,' 'Do not murder,' 'Do not steal,' 'Do not covet,' and whatever other commandment there may be, are summed up in this one rule: 'Love your neighbor as yourself.' Love does no harm to its neighbor. Therefore love is the fulfillment of the law (Rom 13:8–9).

If I speak in the tongues of men and of angels, but have not love, I am only a resounding gong or a clanging cymbal. If I have the gift of prophecy and can fathom all mysteries and all knowledge, and if I have a faith that can move mountains, but have not love, I am nothing. If I give all I possess to the poor and surrender my body to the flames, but have not love, I gain nothing (1 Cor 13:1–3).

If Scripture is our basis for defining love, the above selections show it is more than emotions and even more than action. In *Getting Love Right*, Dallas Willard states that the New Testament claims love is actually a source of action.

Love is . . . a disposition or character: a readiness to act in a certain way under certain conditions . . . If we want to do the things scriptures say, we must change the sources of action in the human self [change the will] . . . We can undertake actions that remove the barriers to love that reside in the various dimensions of the self. They may reside in the will itself, ultimately the root of all the resistance to love: the will as a stubborn resolve to have one's own way, to control others, and to be exalted . . . [we] have to surrender self-will as [our] governing principle, a hardened resolve to have one's own way. [We] will have to yield [our] will to good and to God, and learn to seek what is good for others as well as one's self.

Sadly, one of the largest groups of people in need of truly grasping this are American Christians. I've been shocked by the unwillingness of those who call themselves Christian to reach for any empathy toward those we politically, morally, or religiously disagree with. We have forgotten that our war is against the powers of darkness, not against other people, and while surely darkness can influence others, it's not others themselves we're fighting.

If the follower of Jesus obeys his primary command to love God and others correctly, then everything else becomes moot because it's encompassed within the directive to love—if the church numbering over a billion people loved the other seven billion people on Earth the way we're supposed to, the world would be completely different.

The meaning of life is to love God and others in this way, to wage spiritual war, and to seek the redemption of others and the earth within this rubric of love. Anything else is at best a distraction and at worst an active antagonist against our vocation to love.

8

PUTTING IT ALL TOGETHER

How does the heart learn to rest in knowing it is loved? In part it has to do with being able to perceive God's love in our everyday lives, but it's also more than that. I can see how God has directed, guided, and been kind to me, but it doesn't really move my heart that much.

I think a lot of that has to do with how my feelings were hardened in childhood. There's surely more to it, but deep within me there is something that remains unmoved even when I will its movement. I empathize with those who have fury against a God who seems silent, even silent to the point many conclude he must not exist.

To some extent, I've felt that anger. I've screamed without reply. I've begged for mercy only to be met with harder trials. I've cried at the end of my wits only to be pushed more. I'm not seeking pity because so many people have had infinitely more difficult and painful experiences. I'm just saying I've had a small taste of what it's like.

We're lonely, each one of us, looking to be loved and accepted. Some of us only ever exist as zombies, sucking the life out of others, vainly trying to fill voids within us that another human could never fill. It's one reason why so many marriages fail and we tend to jump from relationship to relationship.

Our society is an existential wasteland without recourse to any actual hope. Our cultural inheritance in the West presents each of us with an uphill battle to fight concerning meaning, truth, faith, trust, hope, and ultimately love.

Perhaps the starting point for those who struggle like me is choosing to accept that we are loved as we are without condition by the Creator of the universe.

MUCH LIKE LOVE, I think hope is, at its heart—contrary to popular belief—a choice more than a feeling. And just like Paul affirms in his first letter to the Corinthian church, along with faith, love and hope are ultimately what lasts (1 Cor 13). I think they are what mark us as human.

It's tempting when depressed to give into nihilism and self-destruction. When we don't actually feel any hope, there's an animal instinct within us that tempts us to give into base urges. When we lose hope, we can convince ourselves there is no meaning beyond the moment, and giving into our impulses and grabbing what little fulfillment we can is the only thing worthwhile we can do.

I've been there. But I know better than that in my heart, as I argue that—deep down—each one of us does, too. There's more to being human than that.

Love is real, and when we choose to hold onto hope, even when we don't feel it, we are clinging to what it truly means to be wholly human—the animal married with the spiritual, the amalgamation of the physical and temporal with the eternal.

Hope keeps us tethered to ultimate reality beyond surface appearances. It reminds us that there are things worth loving, things worth fighting for, things worth dying for. Our lives are more than just deterministic loops, than the sum products of what the chemicals in our brain incline us to do. We prove this by holding onto hope despite all else—when our feelings and our perceptions of our circumstances tell us to give up, but we choose to persist.

But of course our hope is only as valuable as the thing we put our hope in. Many of us hope in the wrong things, and we find ourselves shattered when those things, when those people, fail us. That's why for the Christian, there is truly only one hope, Christ himself. People fail. The church fails. By appearances, even God fails.

But our hope is that, by entering into our existence with us and sharing in our experiences, in our sufferings, in our laughter, and in our tears, Christ has begun to reconcile all the brokenness we see around us with a God who by his triune nature is the source and origin of love. That while we can't explain so much about life and the pain we suffer and the tragedies that befall us, we know God feels it in solidarity through Christ and is working to redeem it all, so one day there will be no more pain, no more tears, no more death.

That is the hope that I imperfectly cling to. And that is the hope that will carry us all through.

ONE OF THE SECRETS to life is that it's not about you or me. It's human to lose sight of that and make life about ourselves, even if it's in the guise of other people—family and loved ones.

I'd forgotten in my worries about what my future was going to look like and what I was going to do with myself that, it's not that that stuff doesn't matter, but that it's not the point. God is the point. God is the focus. The life of living in God's love is what life is supposed to center on. Entering into the eternal community of the Trinity. And having to do so in the company of others, the church.

And that often annoys me, because I'd much rather be on my own most of the time. I'm a paradox in that I usually prefer to be alone, but then I get lonely, and then I avoid the community that would resolve the loneliness.

Community is hard. But a Christian has no choice but to belong to one—it's a command. By nature, a Christian has to be in community with other people.

I'm prone to forget these truths, as we all are prone to forget so many important truths in life as we get distracted by everyday living and our own thoughts.

There's a reason the oldest churches practice liturgy, a set routine to the Christian year and to worship services, and it's in recognition of our need to remember, as well as in acknowledging that we are creatures of habit whether we realize it or not. Weather has seasons that are on repeat throughout our lives, and we live mostly according to routines that we fall into or intentionally develop, so the teaching of the church follows the same pattern as the cyclical nature of life.

We need to be reminded of the truths of God that are central to defining what life is about, and we need to immerse ourselves in the patterns of his life for us in order to become fully who he intends us to be, for his sake because it's what he wants for us, and also our own because what he wants for us will give us the most peace and joy.

The longer I do this thing called Christianity, the more I realize it's about a balance between several factors. Lots of Christians want to make discipleship about one thing: love, grace, faith, social justice, or something else.

But it's a mistake to overemphasize any one characteristic of God or the Christian life. We do the complexity of God an injustice by suggesting he can be, in a sense, summarized according to any one trait. There is danger in doing so because of our temptation to oversimplify, which leads to misunderstanding.

For example, Scripture is clear—and I've made it bluntly clear in this book—that a strong defining characteristic of God is love. First John 4:16 explicitly states, "God is love."

We believe creation itself is a divine act of love within the Trinity; grace is a result of love; mercy is a result of love; the coming of Christ is a result of love. No doubt, love is central—it is also the transforming power of God's love that changes a Christian's heart in order to become more like Christ.

But when defining love, we all bring a lot of baggage to that word that isn't really love at all. The love that is God is almost certainly not what you think about when you think of the word "love." That's really important to understand. Love has been tied to a slew of terms that it's not married to, and consequently it loses its true meaning.

But more than that, as crucial as love is, are we justified in claiming it's *the* defining attribute of God? Granted, Paul states in the ever-popular love chapter of 1 Corinthians 13 that love is the all-defining trait amidst the triumvirate of love, faith, and hope. And I am not at all suggesting we dismiss that.

But what of the other attributes of God? His justice, his holiness? The Old Testament says a ton about these. Justice is the theme of several portions, and of all words used to describe God in Scripture, the only word that is repeated to emphasize its magnitude isn't "love," but "holy."

The phrase "Holy, holy, holy" reappears throughout the Old Testament and at the end of time as depicted in Revelation. The eternal refrain described in that letter as taking place at the throne of God is "Holy, holy, holy is the Lord God Almighty—who was, and is, and is to come" (Rev 4:8).

Holiness is needed to define love, and love is needed to define holiness when one is talking about the nature of God and the nature of the Christian life. It seems to me that, properly, love is included as part of God's holiness, and holiness is impossible without love (without which it becomes self-righteousness). A balance is necessary.

This segues into the primary goal I think a Christian should have in life. Much as I'm hesitant to state a single controlling characteristic of God, I'm cautious about suggesting a single goal for the Christian. But this goal is broad and multi-faceted.

In general, the goal for a Christian is theosis, the process of becoming like God (similar to sanctification).

Oh, that's all. Yeah, as broad as broad can get. Because just as God himself is indescribable in some respects, so would be the process of becoming like him.

But this is Scripture: Christ came to reconcile, reconcile, reconcile. To make humanity—and through humanity all of creation—whole in relation to God.

Because the point of creation and humanity was always to be united intimately with its Creator. As a husband and wife may desire to express their love more fully by creating a new life to grow and share in that love, so the Trinity desires to have all of creation within itself.

One of the underrated benefits of Christ's atoning work is God does us one better than he did at creation. Despite our rebellion, God's reconciliation is far more than just bringing things back to the way they were in the Garden of Eden. It's that and more.

Because in becoming human, Christ wasn't human for just thirty-three years only to return to the form he had prior to that—Hebrews implies that his nature has permanently changed: he is forever human (Heb 7:23–28). The very nature of God has incorporated humanity—God is now and forever part human.

And there's a point to that—God's intent as Scripture states is for Christ to be the firstborn among many brothers and sisters (Rom 8:29). When we begin our reconciliation with God by becoming Christians, the Holy Spirit takes up residence within our hearts and begins a transformative work.

Man, I don't think we emphasize this enough: Christian, God is in you. Right now. This is the beginning of how God is making us like Christ—not like Christ so that we can be some boring, holier-than-thou drone, but so we can join Christ in communion within the Trinity.

Our destiny is to join the Trinity. God wants us, not abstractly in heaven, but intimately within himself. We don't know why and we don't know to what end, but we know that's what God wants.

Humanity is meant to unite with the Trinity. The point of our life now is to let God get us there in a multitude of ways. We are to be growing, through God's love and grace, in Christlikeness. There is a trajectory, there is a point to what we do. Our actions do have consequences.

This journey is not accomplished on our own—it is through grace by the power of Christ that is only accessible through a heart that has been transformed by the love of God. That isn't something you can force or earn.

But, the balance to be held here that is often lost in our Western Christian culture is that grace is not opposed to effort. It is surely opposed to earning. But to effort? No; anathema. We can earn nothing. Our works win us nothing.

But effort itself is requisite for spiritual growth. Not earned growth, but growth brought about through God's grace and compassion, meeting us where we are at God's discretion. The problem is we've equated effort with drudgery, which it's not.

This is the testimony of Scripture when Paul exhorts Christians to be particular people, holy and righteous, exhibiting the fruit of the Spirit, blameless (Eph 4:17—5:20; Gal 5:16-26). This is the testimony of the church. This is the testimony of holy and wonderful saints in the modern era from John Wesley to Dallas Willard. The key is the foundation of a heart transformed by love, resting in grace.

Ideally, our effort doesn't feel like work because it's flowing as a result of our utter love and thankfulness toward God. But not all Christians feel this way, and it's a grace of God to receive this sense. Regardless, the paradox is, wherever our heart is on the spectrum of transformation, we are still called to give effort no matter how it feels to us. Because asking God for help and seeking to have our hearts more fully transformed by actively resting or focusing on what Christ has done, is, well, effort.

As a good friend once said, it's likely a good idea if we recognize that our hearts and lives aren't where they need to be to borrow the prayers—the words—of brothers and sisters gone on before us who were farther down the line of maturity than we are. That is the value of liturgy, the value of reciting prayer and reading the saints—to saturate ourselves in what they knew and who they were till it becomes our own.

ONE OF MY FAVORITE theologians is Dietrich Bonhoeffer, a relatively famous Christian known for his tangential affiliation with the Valkyrie plot to assassinate Adolf Hitler in 1944 which resulted in his execution by the Nazi State. One of Bonhoeffer's most popular books is a work whose English title is *The Cost of Discipleship*, though in German it is simply called *Discipleship*.

This book is Bonhoeffer's take on what it means to follow Christ, written in 1937 in the midst of the rise of Nazism in Germany. His ideas are that much more powerful when taken within this context and against this backdrop.

One of the core distinctions is between what Bonhoeffer calls "cheap" and "costly" grace. "Cheap grace is the preaching of forgiveness without requiring repentance, baptism without church discipline. Communion without confession. Cheap grace is grace without discipleship, grace without the cross, grace without Jesus Christ," Bonhoeffer wrote.

In contrast, "Costly grace confronts us as a gracious call to follow Jesus, it comes as a word of forgiveness to the broken spirit and the contrite heart. It is costly because it compels a man to submit to the yoke of Christ and follow him; it is grace because Jesus says: 'My yoke is easy and my burden is light.'"

I quote Bonhoeffer here because I've come to a similar conclusion about Christianity and remembered Bonhoeffer came to it first eighty years ago (credit where credit is due): it is hard to be a Christian. Really hard. Specifically, I mean hard as a lifelong commitment, not as a single moment in time.

We all have emotional highs and lows, and during the heights when grace seems to flow abundantly and freely, relatively speaking it is quite easy to be a Christian. But during the valleys of life, it can be incredibly difficult. Depending on the depths of those valleys and the amount of time they last, people can and do sometimes lose their faith and stop identifying as Christian.

This is a hard reality and one that is not easy or popular to write about. Having grown up in a Christian home and environment, it's not something that I recall ever being discussed. That's much to our detriment as our silence on the matter can suggest to those who are struggling that their struggles in faith are not normal.

When I claim that being a Christian is difficult, I mean it's hard for those who are intentionally trying to live as a Christian. That means someone who is actively attempting to live out a life in submission to Christ. This is sadly in contrast to people who consider themselves to be Christian because they intellectually believe certain doctrines but in actuality are not practicing disciples of Christ.

Ouch. Allow me to unpack that. Go back to Bonhoeffer: cheap grace—forgiveness without repentance; baptism without discipline; Communion without confession. I dare suggest this is where the majority of Americans who identify as Christian actually are. They believe in their heads, but they are still the gods of their own lives.

Don't get me wrong, we all struggle with this. We all grab control of our lives back from God from time to time. But many of us never actually make the attempt to submit ourselves to God in the first place.

To be a disciple of Christ is to live life differently than the rest of the world. Cheap grace doesn't work. It isn't really grace. Costly grace is the only real grace, and it comes, as the name suggests, at a cost.

That cost is the death of our old self, of the way of life that we see everyone else living broadcast to us continuously through music, movies, radio, television, billboards, social media, internet ads, pornography, newspapers, downtown in cities, and a million other mediums. To be a Christian is to determine to say no to the world.

It allows for mistakes along the way. It allows us to fall short and requires us to ask for more grace and forgiveness. It demands we realize our complete inadequacy in and of ourselves, an epiphany that we need a savior because we can't do any of this stuff on our own, that the indwelling of the Holy Spirit is the only way we will ever have any successes—and those only through his power, his might, and his faithfulness.

But it does not allow for my life to be *my life*, fitting God in around the edges. That's only achieved through surrender to him. By us letting go and allowing him lordship over our lives, allowing him to remake them in his image according to his ways.

That is the personal meaning of the cross for the Christian. We pick up our cross and follow him, which is a daily (hourly) death to our ways and surrender to his ways.

We stumble. But we get up. We fall down. But we get up. We keep going. We finish this race. It's a marathon, not a sprint.

A friend once told me so much of Paul's letters in the New Testament can be summarized in one phrase: don't give up. Because we want to. It's hard. The world seems like it's having so much fun a lot of the time.

But like the disciples in the gospels, Christians realize deep down that not only is the way of the world ultimately meaningless, but that it leads to death. Death in a thousand different ways—to love, to life, to freedom, to truth, to dignity, to honor, to loyalty, to faith, to hope.

The world offers joy and fun that is fleeting and cheap, but I know deep down that it is death. Other religions, other philosophies, they have some elements of truth and much wisdom, but they are not Truth, which is a person.

Only one has the words that resonate deep inside us, in places that speak to our hearts, minds, and souls. Where else would we go, Lord? We submit ourselves to you, warts and all, struggles and all, and ask for your help in getting us through this race to the finish line.

That is the cost of being a Christian.

A RECENT TURNING POINT for me hasn't come from me sucking up my own inner strength and resolving to try my hardest to fight my battles against fear. Ironically enough, it came when I gave up.

I asked for God's help in guiding me to whittle away at all the various fears I've had in life to the root—just what was at the base of the panic I've suffered from when I felt helpless? It became clear to me that, in different ways, the common denominator in my bouts with panic has been the feeling of being trapped.

As a boy, I felt trapped by my own thoughts—I worked myself up into a panic frenzy that made me sick, and I felt completely helpless and stuck in misery because there was no way to free myself from my own mind short of death.

In my early twenties after my brief foray in ministry, I felt trapped by my own inadequacies and shortcomings and allowed myself to short-circuit and implode in order to escape.

In my late-twenties, I felt trapped when I was scared to death that I might lose custody of my daughter—I had no control over the situation and was completely at the mercy of the decisions of others.

In my early thirties, I allowed the subconscious fear of being trapped to prevent me from walking down paths God had called me to, paths I wasn't sure about in part because I didn't want to know clearly whether God had called me to something that could lead me into feeling . . . trapped.

While I've wanted to be married and haven't let my fears get in the way of seeking marriage in the past, part of me has been scared to death that I'd find myself in a relationship that—for any number of potential reasons—would leave me miserable, and yet, that whole "till death do us part" bit is something I take pretty seriously, so, hey, another way to be trapped.

When God led me to this realization, I had one of those moments of clarity you sometimes hear about, and it wasn't a revolutionary thought at all, but it suddenly struck home in my heart: external situations don't matter.

Wait. What?

"Is Christ in you? The Holy Spirit, God himself—is he in you?"

Yes?

"Then the situations you find yourself in don't matter. It's impossible for you to be trapped."

But, sure I can, whe—

"No. You can be in the most hopeless, painful, and despairing place in the external world, where you are 'stuck' in all the ways a person can be. But *you*, David . . . in Christ, *you* cannot be trapped. Because Christ is in you, and your ultimate reality is in him, you cannot possibly be trapped by anything, no matter what the external circumstance."

That stirred something in me. I don't know if it stirs anything in you—you're different from me, and God speaks to each of us in different ways and at different times.

But don't you see, that has to be what the saints like Paul and Silas knew when they sang hymns of praise in the midst of being chained in prison? Their reality, their true reality, was centered in Christ in them—what happens externally, it doesn't make it meaningless or unimportant, but it puts it into context.

And I know I'm trying to explain in words what can only be grasped by the heart, and these are clichéd words I've heard in different variations from several Christians my whole life: "My life is in Christ," "My joy is in the Lord," yadda, yadda, yadda. The words *are* meaningless without a context, and that context has to come from your heart understanding something words by themselves can't express.

Because Christ lives in me, I cannot be trapped. When my body physically reacts to stress in old patterns that would summon panic, I can remind it ("renew my mind" [Rom 12:2]) that, no, that's an old learned habit that can—that will—be changed: I cannot be trapped, because the Spirit in me means, truly, that I am free.

But what if in this freedom I venture forth and only stumble upon the same old failings I've experienced so many times before? I know how weak I am. I know how imperfect. I know my flaws, my vices. I know how I've failed doing God's work before, more than once, and how I've failed just doing my own thing, more than once.

So much of that failure was self-induced, though, wasn't it? I had expectations for myself that weren't being met, or I let other people's expectations for me become the way in which I judged my success. The truth is, as long as I am being the kind of person God made me to be, I cannot be a failure.

Nothing else is a litmus test for success. Just me being who I was created to be. And I know who that guy is. Mostly. I've hidden from him a lot, unintentionally. I let fear, failure, and shame shut him up behind closed doors in my heart.

But there is no condemnation. No regrets. God will use all my failures, all my struggles, all my heartaches, and he will use them to help others be free, just as he is freeing me.

MANY OF MY EMOTIONAL and spiritual struggles come from hurts concerning fatherhood. One of the central issues of my Christian life has been an inability to receive the love of God the Father. My heart just hasn't known how. I couldn't make it. I knew the right answers in my head, but my heart was a cold stone.

I knew the truths of the Father's love for humanity as depicted in Scripture. But it hadn't penetrated my heart. Because I didn't really believe it, because I'd never really experienced anything like it.

I needed a father to affirm me and tell me I was strong, loved, capable, powerful, and would be victorious when the demons of depression and panic attacked me as a small boy. My dad did his best, but affirmations weren't really in his wheelhouse having grown up in the Great Depression. And God the Father didn't respond in a way I could understand.

I don't agree with everything author John Eldredge says and writes, but I think he gets some critically important things right. In his book *Fathered by God*, which is tailored for men but I think applies equally well for women in most regards, he points out several helpful truths.

He says every man has a core question regarding existence, and in essence that question is, "Do I have what it takes?" Eldredge states, though, that "Before and beneath that Question and a man's search for validation lies a deeper need—to know that he is prized, delighted in, that he is the beloved son. Our need for a father's love."

Yet Eldredge then accurately points out the truth at the heart of many of our experiences:

> You are the son of a kind, strong, and engaged Father . . . [but] this is perhaps the hardest thing for us to believe—really believe, down deep in our hearts, so that it changes us forever, changes the way we approach each day . . . I believe this is the core issue of our shared dilemma as men. We just don't believe it. Our core assumptions about the world boil down to this: we are on our own to make life work. We are not watched over. We are not cared for . . . When we are hit with a problem, we have to figure it out ourselves, or just take the hit. If anything good is going to come our way, we're the ones who are going to have to arrange for it. Many of us have called upon God as Father, but, frankly, he doesn't seem to have heard. We're not sure why . . . Whatever the reason, our experience of this world has framed our approach to life. We believe we are fatherless.

Yeah. That's me. Spot on.

> A [child] . . . yearns to know he is adored. Uniquely. That he holds a special place in [a] father's heart, a place no one and nothing else can rival. Without this certainty down in the core of his being, the [child] will misinterpret the stages and lessons that are to come . . . tests and challenges often feel to [adults] like a form of rejection or coldheartedness on the part of God, because [we] do not first know in [our] heart of hearts that [we are] the beloved son . . . Without this bedrock of affirmation, this core of assurance, [we] will move unsteadily through the rest of life.

I hope to impart this deep love to my daughter. In hindsight, I can tell many of the choices I've made as an adult have been the result of brokenness experienced as a child. My wrestling with a major in college was, really, an attempt at determining the best course of study that would result in receiving some form of affirmation—from society, I guess—that would serve as a kind of drug to numb the void in my soul where a father's abiding love and acceptance should have been.

Failing in multiple ways to travel a path where I would receive metaphorical resounding applause, I've kind of just muddled through in life, getting by, as the vast majority of us do. There is no victory in life lived this way, only an abject acceptance that the best any of us can do is survive, a belief that, for me, goes back deep into my family heritage for generations.

But the Christian belief is in a life that is abundant, not so much in material possessions, but in love and joy. And bare-minimum survival does not equate to abundance.

A lot of the themes Eldredge repeats throughout his book involve adventure, exploration, and a sense of wonder. As I read it, I found myself getting annoyed whenever I came across yet another reference to these types of things because they haven't been feelings I'd experienced in a long time. So I thought back to my childhood, trying to recall the last time I felt wonder at the world, and I tapped back into the emotions associated with my love for history.

I remembered hunting for arrowheads on the playground at school. I remembered playing with neighborhood friends, exploring the vast open pastures and forests where we grew up. Taking trips into sinkholes, taking backwoods routes after school on our way to the library. Writing a short book on the history of my hometown in the fifth grade.

So, I decided to go back to where I started. I got in my car, drove past my parents' house where I grew up, and went down to the now-abandoned railroad tracks I walked with my dad as a boy.

And I walked. And I explored. And I found God.

There he was as my heart rediscovered what intrigued me as a boy. He was in the air around those tracks, whispering through the voices of the past around train stops now long reclaimed by forest.

He was in the beautiful foliage that covered the tracks; in the cry of the hawk I heard in the sky; in the dampness of my skin; in my heart.

I'm reminded of a scene from *Chariots of Fire*. The movie tells the tale of the 1924 Olympic track team from the United Kingdom, and one of the main characters is Eric Liddell, a Christian who runs for joy and to bring God glory.

Liddell's family serve as missionaries in China, and it's this commitment that dominates most of his life. Yet, he is also committed to running, much to the disapproval of his sister, Jennie, who thinks it's a distraction from what's truly important.

During his Olympic training, Liddell accidentally misses a prayer meeting, and Jennie confronts him, accusing him of not caring about God. He reassures her he intends to fulfill his commitment to the mission, and that in fact he runs because of God, not in spite of him, and to not run would be to dishonor him.

He says, "I believe that God made me for a purpose. But he also made me fast, and when I run, I feel his pleasure."

This exchange, coupled with the race Liddell ultimately runs at the Olympic Games, never fails to bring me to tears. This man knows God gave him a gift, and when he participates in what God gave him, he feels his pleasure. It moves me deeply.

God has given each of us something in which we, too, can feel his joy. Where we can experience his love, his romancing of us.

It's different for many of us, tailored to who we are as people. For me, when I dig into history, when I try to discover the stories of people long forgotten and bring them back to life, when I walk around a place where others have tread hundreds or thousands of years before, I feel his pleasure.

DENOUEMENT

My great-grandfather's headstone is too heavy to carry by hand now that it's back in one piece, so my cousin helps me load it onto a dolly from the trunk of my rental car, and I wheel it slowly over bumpy terrain back to its Ohio resting place.

It's bright white now except for the dull grey color of the dried mortar covering the sealed crack, and the sun is glistening off it on a cool September day.

The hole where I dug the footer up over a year ago is thankfully not filled in, just slightly overgrown with grass.

I shovel a small foundation of crushed gravel on the bottom of the hole, then put the footer back in the place it had been for over a century.

My cousin and I guide the headstone into the slot on the top of the footer, then I carefully attempt to level it while she holds it steady. Once satisfied, we pour wet mortar around the edges of the slot so it flows down into the empty spaces to dry and hold the stone firmly in place. Two pieces of rebar then brace the headstone so it stays level while the mortar dries.

I sit in the grass and look at the result of the effort. I'm still a little disappointed I wasn't able to match the mortar color for the crack to the sandstone's natural white, but otherwise I think the only giveaway to the stone being 160-years-old is the date written on it. It looks great. I continue to pray that the seal holds when winter, snow, and ice come.

I think about my great-grandfather. I wish I knew more about him. I realize I almost certainly never will, at least on this side of eternity.

Did he know much about family tradition from generations before, or had it already begun to be forgotten? Was he a kind man? What were his dreams, his hopes, his aspirations?

I wonder for how long his loved ones came to visit his grave, and I wonder when they stopped. Did his children ever visit as adults, or were they too young when he passed to feel a sense of responsibility to honor him? Did his widow ever come, or did she put that part of her life completely behind her when she remarried?

How long did it take for memory of his existence to be all but forgotten?

I wish there was something more I could do to honor him and all those who came before who have nothing tangible left to mark their existence.

But in a real sense, by living my life and contributing small brush strokes to the broad canvas that is the portrait of a family, I do just that.

While all the details of our family saga have been lost to time, it nonetheless continues to live on in my cousins, my parents, my brother, my nieces, my daughter, and me.

In that sense, our story never ends. And, it's part of something far bigger than just a narrative of our particular family.

It impacts the lives of those all around us and informs the tales of those who follow. We drastically affect the Story the Grand Author himself is writing—the one that binds all others together—in ways we could never guess or hope for.

And rest in knowing you are precious to him, your life is necessary and a gift to others, and you will never fade from his memory.